Women
and
Urban Society

URBAN STUDIES INFORMATION GUIDE SERIES

Series Editor: Thomas P. Murphy, Director, Institute for Urban Studies at the University of Maryland, College Park (on leave) and Director of the Federal Executive Institute, Charlottesville, Virginia

Also in this series:

SUBURBIA—*Edited by Joseph Zikmund II and Deborah Ellis Dennis*

URBAN COMMUNITY—*Edited by Anthony J. Filipovitch and Earl J. Reeves*

URBAN DECISION MAKING: THE BASIS FOR ANALYSIS—*Edited by Mark Drucker**

URBAN EDUCATION—*Edited by George E. Spear and Donald W. Mocker*

URBAN FISCAL POLICY AND ADMINISTRATION—*Edited by John L. Mikesell and Jerry L. McCaffery**

URBAN HOUSING: PUBLIC AND PRIVATE—*Edited by John E. Rouse, Jr.*

URBAN INDICATORS—*Edited by Thomas P. Murphy**

URBAN LAW—*Edited by Thomas P. Murphy**

URBAN MANAGEMENT—*Edited by Bernard H. Ross*

URBAN PLANNING—*Edited by Ernest R. Alexander, Anthony J. Catanese, and David S. Sawicki*

URBAN POLICY—*Edited by Dennis J. Palumbo and George Taylor*

URBAN POLITICS—*Edited by Thomas P. Murphy*

*in preparation

The above series is part of the
GALE INFORMATION GUIDE LIBRARY

The Library consists of a number of separate series of guides covering major areas in the social sciences, humanities, and current affairs.

General Editor: Paul Wasserman, Professor and former Dean, School of Library and Information Services, University of Maryland

Managing Editor: Denise Allard Adzigian, Gale Research Company

Women
and
Urban Society

A GUIDE TO INFORMATION SOURCES

Volume 7 in the Urban Studies Information Guide Series

Hasia R. Diner

Fellow
Radcliffe Institute for Independent Study
Cambridge, Massachusetts

Gale Research Company
Book Tower, Detroit, Michigan 48226

Library of Congress Cataloging in Publication Data

Diner, Hasia R
    Women and urban society.

    (Urban studies information guide series; v. 7)
    Bibliography: p. 138
    Includes indexes.
    1. Women—Bibliography. 2. Urbanization—Bibliography. 3. City
and town life—Bibliography. 4. Sociology, Urban—Bibliography.
I. Title. II. Series.
Z7961.D55   [HQ1154]   016.30141'2   78-13109
ISBN 0-8103-1425-8

VITA

Hasia R. Diner is a fellow at the Radcliffe Institute for Independent Study in Cambridge, Massachusetts. She was previously a visiting professor in the department of history at Goucher College in Towson, Maryland. She received her B.A. in history from the University of Wisconsin in 1968; her M.A.T. in history from the University of Chicago in 1970; and Ph.D. in history from the University of Illinois in 1975. She has taught at George Washington University, the University of Maryland, and Federal City College.

Diner's publications include: IN THE ALMOST PROMISED LAND: AMERICAN JEWS AND BLACKS, 1915-1935; and "Teapot Dome, 1924" in CONGRESS INVESTIGATES: A DOCUMENTED HISTORY. 1792-1974.

CONTENTS

INTRODUCTION

In his classic essay "Urbanism as a Way of Life" (1938), sociologist Louis
Wirth suggested that cities were not "conducive to the traditional family,"
and that in many American cities, "women predominate numerically over
men." He noted that "the failure of the urban population to reproduce itself
appears to be a biological consequence of a combination of factors in the
complex of urban life." Urban mothers, he asserted, "are likely to be employed, . . . marriage tends to be postponed, and the proportion of single
and unattached people is greater" in cities than in rural areas. With the
breakdown of traditional family obligations, Wirth observed unhappily, the
"individual members pursue their own diverging interests in their vocational,
educational, religious, recreational, and political life." Wirth's interest in
the social life of cities followed his exposure to the pioneering work in urban
sociology of his mentors at the University of Chicago--W.I. Thomas, Robert
Park, and Ernest Burgess. These scholars were influenced by the conditions
of urban growth and urban development occurring in Chicago. What they in
fact observed was an advanced stage of urbanization in the United States.
Their focus was American urban adjustment, and Wirth's work in general,
and his now-famous essay, used the American city of the pre-World War II
years as the basis for sweeping generalizations.

In the nearly forty years since Wirth published this provocative and seminal
essay, numerous scholars have evaluated the validity of Wirth's theory in
particular social settings. Others, without specific reference to the Wirth
essay, have broadened our knowledge of the way in which urbanization affects women and family structures. The bulk of this literature addresses five
general issues: (1) women and the process of urban migration and accommodation to the urban environment; (2) women and the urban family; (3) urban
fertility patterns; (4) female employment in urban society; and (5) the psychological and social implications of urbanization for women. This bibliography contains sections on each of these issues, and also a sparser section on
the images and attitudes towards urban women.

Students of rural-urban migration and its consequences have been primarily
interested in the relative numbers of men and women who migrate to cities
and in the sex composition of various urban areas. They have discovered

important regional patterns. Western countries generally find women outnumbering men in cities, and clearly predominating among the most recent migrants from the countryside to city. Females exceed men even more heavily among migrants to Latin American cities. In Africa and Asia, the pattern is reversed. Especially in Africa, women are infrequent urban migrants and are distinct minorities among urban dwellers. The only exception on these continents is the Philippines which adheres closely to the Latin American model. Much of the literature speculates on the significance of this overwhelming male dominance for urban life in Africa and Asia. Much of it also analyzes the consequences for women of being a numerical majority or minority, particularly as that condition affects the process of female integration into the urban environment. Studies of this sort frequently concern themselves with patterns of female migration, where they deviate from male patterns, and the particular characteristics of those women who move to cities, as opposed to those who remain in traditional, rural areas.

Urban family structure is perhaps the most thoroughly treated subject in the whole literature of urbanization and women. Scholars have looked at family composition in a wide variety of societies to determine how the membership of urban families differs from that of rural families, how extended families give way to conjugal families, and how in many societies a matriarchal household replaces a patriarchal one. Almost all of these studies show that urbanization has profoundly changed family relations, and many conclude that the nuclear unit has become the predominant urban form, throwing husband and wife into closer interaction with each other. Some scholars see this optimistically as a democratizing development, while others insist that it has increased the isolation and dependence of the urban woman. Other family practices which have attracted research include childbirth and breast feeding in cities, child-rearing patterns, and the changes in marriage negotiations and courtship in the urban setting. There is also a modest literature on urban prostitution. Of the various world regions, African family patterns in the city have by far attracted the greatest attention.

Intimately linked to questions of women's urban status is the issue of urban fertility, a matter of paramount importance to social policy. These studies, most of them highly quantitative and technical, seek to discover if urban residence affects fertility by examining the effect on fertility rates of urban characteristics like education for women, availability of contraceptives, and employment. Again important regional variations appear. In industrialized nations fertility falls off dramatically with urbanization. In India, on the other hand, the researchers have concluded that urban migration has had no effect whatsoever on the rates of childbearing.

Scholars have posed a variety of questions regarding women's employment in cities and its consequences, besides the aforementioned issue of its impact on fertility. Much of the literature has explored the job opportunities which lure women to the city, although some scholars argue that rural-urban migration severely narrows women's economic sphere. In cities with high rates of maternal employment, researchers have explored the ways women coordinate their domestic and occupational roles. Because African women have assumed the economic roles of traders and controllers of the market, scholars have been especially intrigued with the development of the female market monopoly in Africa, how it functions, and how it affects urban African family life. Social scientists generally agree that employment opportunities for women in most countries increase in the city, but many also stress the continuing cycle of discrimination against women in the job market.

Because of such discrimination and the isolation of city life, urban women have bonded together in formal and informal associations. Scholars have examined several aspects of social interaction among urban women. Although the literature on this problem is varied and lacks a central focus, certain aspects of it stand out. These include studies of women's emotional and psychological adjustment to city life, their activities outside the immediate family other than employment, their informal social networks, and their participation in urban politics and reform movements. Many of the writers here have argued over whether the urban environment has been a liberating or constricting influence on women.

Finally, a small but provocative body of literature notes that most societies experiencing the tensions of urbanization and modernization tend to develop negative images of urban women. Often depicted as "free" and independent, frequently immoral, women shoulder the blame for the changing social and cultural patterns which men find unsettling.

The vast bulk of the literature has been written since World War II. Very few studies from the period before the 1940s stand out as noteworthy or valid. The only exceptions are some of the products of the Chicago school of sociology of Thomas, Park, Burgess, Wirth, and E. Franklin Frazier. These scholars focused on the adjustment to urban life contemporary with their own writing. Thus they were primarily interested in the cities of the United States, as they experienced vast influxes of immigrants from abroad and accepted thousands of newcomers from the American countryside.

The largest number of entries in this bibliography are also contemporary. Writing since the 1940s, the scholars have primarily chosen to analyze women in those societies undergoing urbanization. Thus the literature is much more heavily weighted toward studies of Africa, Asia, and Latin America than toward studies of the United States, Eastern or Western Europe. Among scholars in the various social science disciplines, sociologists have continued to do the most research on the impact of urban life on women. The subject has also attracted the attention of many demographers, anthropologists, and political scientists. To a lesser degree we have the fruits of the research of economists and psychologists. The literature is strikingly deficient in historic analysis. The vast majority of the studies have been and continue to be contemporary, and scholars have apparently found it easier to study women in urban societies where urbanization is still occurring dramatically. What seems to be needed therefore are more studies comparing these societies with advanced industrial societies which underwent these changes in the nineteenth century. Data on these societies will have to be gleaned from the fragmentary historic records.

Section I

WOMEN AND URBANIZATION

Section I includes entries which deal with the sex composition of cities, the sex composition of the streams of urban migrants, and the relationship of women to the process of urban migration and urbanization.

Banton, Michael P. WEST AFRICAN CITY: A STUDY OF TRIBAL LIFE IN FREETOWN. London: Oxford University Press, 1957. 228 p.

Based on a 1953 sample survey and published for the International African Institute, this study points out that women migrate and settle in Freetown, Sierra Leone, in equal numbers to men. The author links this demographic characteristic with the decline of polygamy in Freetown. He also notes that women in cities exhibit greater independence than in rural, traditional societies.

Bascom, William R. "Some Aspects of Yoruba Urbanism." AMERICAN AN-THROPOLOGIST 64 (August 1962): 699-709.

The Yoruba are the most urban of all African tribes. Bascom views various aspects of urban social structure of the Yoruba in Nigeria. Looking at a number of cities where the Yoruba cluster, the author finds that there is a range of sex ratios, but that despite differences, all cities show a strikingly higher percentage of men than women among the urban residents.

Butterworth, Douglass [S.]. "Rural-Urban Migration and Microdemography: A Case Study from Mexico." URBAN ANTHROPOLOGY 4 (Fall 1975): 265-83.

Age data from the Mexican national censuses show that the community of Tilantongo, Oaxaca, has a high fertility ratio, relatively large cohorts in the young adult ages, and a balanced sex ratio, which might suggest a growing population. Yet, after examining vital data and data from previous censuses, it is obvious that the community has been experiencing an intense out-migration. A special census conducted by the author provides some leads about the selectivity of the migration patterns which resulted in the observed age-sex structure.

1

Women and Urbanization

_____ . "A Study of the Urbanization Process among the Mixtec Migrants from Tilantonso in Mexico City." AMERICA INDIGENA 22 (August 1962): 257-74.

In a fairly descriptive article on Mixtec Indian adjustment to urban life, the author notes that very few of the migrants are unmarried women, except for those who are accompanying their parents. The author implies that the process of urbanization has a more profound impact on the lives of men, using evidence such as changes in clothing patterns. Women shed some of their rural peasant garb, while men shed all of it.

Caldwell, John Charles. AFRICAN RURAL-URBAN MIGRATION: THE MOVEMENT TO GHANA'S TOWNS. Canberra: Australian National University Press, 1969. 258 p.

Part of the study was based on interviews with migrants. Respondents give only qualified support for the migration of women to cities. Most fear that women in cities are subject to the temptation to drift into prostitution. Only one-tenth of the interviewees justify unequivocally the movement of women away from traditional, rural life. Most respondents, both male and female, believe that the differences between urban and rural life were greater for women than men. Ghana's cities have a large male surplus.

Church, Roy A. ECONOMIC AND SOCIAL CHANGE IN A MIDLAND TOWN: VICTORIAN NOTTINGHAM, 1815-1900. London: Frank Cass, 1966. 409 p.

There was a constant increase in the number of women in Nottingham between 1811 and 1834. Through 1861 women outnumbered men by three to four thousand. After 1861 the excess of females continued to rise. The continuous flow of women was due to the employment opportunities for women in local trades.

Cohen, Abner. CUSTOM AND POLITICS IN URBAN AFRICA: A STUDY OF HAUSA MIGRANTS IN YORUBA TOWNS. London: Routledge and Kegan Paul, 1969. 252 p.

The author begins with the generalization that sociologists have measured the stability or instability of African migrant communities by their male-female proportion. Hausa urban migrants have been considered the most stabilized urban group because of the proportion of women to men, calculated at 400 to 1,000. More recent research, however, indicates that women do not migrate to cities in as large numbers as previously estimated.

Darlow, Mary. "The African Tribeswoman in Northern Rhodesia." AFRICAN WOMEN 1 (December 1955): 57-59.

2

Few girls between the ages ten and fifteen are found in the urban areas, even though the author estimates that the cities contain a higher proportion of young married women than does the countryside. Similarly, the urban population centers contain very few women over the age of forty. The author believes that the young African women in the city lack the traditional guidance which older women could provide. Although women make up one-third of the urban population, they are concentrated in the twenty- to forty-year age bracket. The author details the types of social services and recreational activities available to these young women.

Folger, John, and Rowan, John. "Migration and Marital Status in Ten Southeastern Cities." SOCIAL FORCES 32 (December 1953): 178-85.

The authors used information from the special census tabulations of the United States 1940 Census to test the hypothesis that single and divorced or widowed individuals are more likely to migrate than married people. The authors found that widowed and divorced women generally migrated less frequently from cities to less urban areas. Urban locations seemed to be more attractive to these women. Among migrants to urban places, females widowed and divorced appeared in large numbers. Similarly, farms, villages, and suburban areas did not attract single women.

Gibson, Jeffry Royle. "A Demographic Analysis of Urbanization: Evolution of a System of Cities in Honduras, El Salvador, and Costa Rica." Ph.D. Dissertation, Cornell University, 1970.

Using 1960s published census data and official statistics of these Central American countries, supplemented with earlier census material and historical data, the author breaks out the data on sex ratio, age-sex structure, and population movements. One hypothesis he offers is that a social system with low levels of industrialization and increased employment opportunities for female workers should produce an inverse relationship between sex ratio and size of place. This hypothesis is borne out with a few exceptions.

González, Nancy L. Solien. BLACK CARIB HOUSEHOLD STRUCTURE: A STUDY OF MIGRATION AND MODERNIZATION. Seattle: University of Washington Press, 1969. 163 p.

In cities where there is a sex imbalance, a consanguineal family system appears. This study of Livingston, Guatemala, where women outnumber men, poses that the nucleus of this type of family is the mother and her child. This dyad as nucleus seems to be intimately related to the process of urbanization and modernization and can be found in a whole range of societies. This type of family structure provides an alternative form of domestic life for migratory, low-income, wage-earning women who are making their first contacts with westernization.

Gore, Madhav Sadashiv. INMIGRANTS AND NEIGHBOURHOODS: TWO ASPECTS OF LIFE IN A METROPOLITAN CITY. Bombay: Tata Institute of Social Sciences, 1970. 303 p.

This study of Bombay points to an acute scarcity of women. Many of the male migrants to Bombay leave their wives in rural villages for two reasons: Bombay has a lack of adequate, decent housing to accommodate migrant families; and male urban migrants need to leave their wives behind to preserve and protect their property.

Gugler, Josef. "The Second Sex in Town." CANADIAN JOURNAL OF AFRICAN STUDIES 6 (1972): 289-302.

An increasing number of women are attracted to the fast-growing sub-Saharan African cities. This movement to urban areas has released women from some traditional constraints on their behavior. This stream of women into the cities would be even greater if the urban economies offered women the potential to earn enough money that would in turn compensate for the loss of their rural incomes. The author notes that there are two significant areas of policy formation which affect women: (1) women's access to education and employment, and (2) the position of the woman within the family. The author concludes that urban sex discrimination keeps women from joining their husbands in the cities, and is therefore responsible for the separation of families.

_____. "Urbanization in East Africa." In SOCIAL CHANGE IN EASTERN AFRICA, edited by Peter Rigby, pp. 53-66. Kampala, Uganda: Makerere Institute of Social Research, 1969.

Throughout East Africa there is a heavy preponderance of men among urban dwellers. While there is some variation in many East African cities, the masculine character of the urban populations still holds.

Gulick, Margaret E., and Gulick, John. "Migrant and Native Married Women in the Iranian City of Isfahan." ANTHROPOLOGICAL QUARTERLY 49 (January 1976): 53-61.

This study compares migrant and city native women. The 63 migrants and the 102 natives studied were of the same average age (26) and were married the same average number of years (11). The authors found many similarities between these two groups of women: age at marriage (15.5 for the native and 14.3 for the migrants), number of pregnancies (5.5 and 4.9), and number of living children (3.6 and 3.3). The two groups of women had similar types of household structures and both groups had frequent contact with kin. Among the differences presented the researchers note that the native women are less frequently illiterate. Native women prefer fewer children, and fewer natives than migrants had never practiced some form of contraception. Native women have greater hopes for the education of their daughters. The authors, however, minimize the influence of the urban environment on these differences. More importantly, the authors attribute the similarities, which they saw as more salient, to the pattern of female urban migration with their husbands from a domestically oriented, sex-segregated rural environment to a protected domestic environment within the city--an environment that was not all that different from the one they had left in the country.

Gutkind, Peter Claus Wolfgang. "African Urban Marriage and Family Life: A Note on Some Social and Demographic Characteristics from Kampala, Uganda." BULLETIN DE L'INSTITUT FONDAMENTAL D'AFRIQUE NOIR 25 (July-October 1963): 266-87.

This article is based on data from the Urban Social Survey, conducted in 1953-55, which includes information on 3,493 individuals. The author states that the urban-rural dichotomy, especially in relation to family structure, has been overstated. He finds that young children of urban dwellers spend a considerable amount of time in rural areas, away from their parents--especially away from their urban fathers. African urbanism tends to find a predominant number of young women among the female population, and there are few significant differences between the rural and urban birth rates.

_____. URBAN ANTHROPOLOGY: PERSPECTIVES ON "THIRD WORLD" URBANISATION AND URBANISM. Studies of Developing Nations, vol. 15. Assen, Netherlands: Van Gorcum, 1974. 270 p.

This interpretive study asserts that the most salient features of urban marriage patterns in Africa and of urban family life are its demographic characteristics. The stream of migrants to the cities is heavily comprised of young men. These men return to rural areas to find wives. Those women who have migrated are usually young and unattached. They are derisively known as "town women."

Hart, Donn V. "Philippine Rural-Urban Migration: A View from Caticugan, A Bisayan Village." BEHAVIOR SCIENCE NOTES 6 (1971): 103-37.

The central question raised here is why peasants migrate to the city, either temporarily or permanently. Among the factors considered was sex. Based on data collected between 1951 and 1965, the article indicates that the migration is at first heavily male. This is followed by a shift in sex ratios among the urban migrants, so that in the most recent years cities have been more attractive to women than men. Thus Philippine urban migration patterns are closer to European patterns during the Industrial Revolution than to other lands in Southeast Asia. The lure of the cities for women is related to the expansion of manufacturing jobs which are considered women's work, as well as the increase of opportunities in secretarial work, teaching, and nursing. The author concludes that the influence of American ideas has worked towards equalizing sex roles.

Houser, Philip Morris. "Demographic Aspects of Urbanization in Latin America." In his URBANIZATION IN LATIN AMERICA, pp. 91-117. New York: Population Branch, Bureau of Social Affairs, United Nations, 1961.

Sponsored by UNESCO, this study asserts that in all the Latin American countries studied, there is a low sex ratio. The author also notes that those Latin American cities have a lower fertility rate than the rural areas. This is in part due to the preponderance of females in the rural-urban migration. The lower urban fertility is clearly not related to the degree of urbanization within the country as a whole. The urban areas of Latin America have a significantly higher number of widows than widowers.

International Population Conference. PROCEEDINGS. New York, 1961. London: UNESCO, 1963.

The following papers deal with the subject of women in the process of urban migration and urbanization:

Arias, B. Jorge. "Internal Migration in Guatemala." Pp. 395-404.

Internal, urban movement in Guatemala is predominantly female.

Ducoff, Louis J. "The Migrant Population of a Metropolitan Area in a Developing Country: A Preliminary Report on a Case Study of San Salvador." Pp. 428-36.

Women predominate as urban migrants, since employment opportunities for women in rural areas are severely limited. Like many South American and Central American cities, San Salvador is marked by a large number of low-skill, low-productivity jobs in domestic service and petty commerce which attract rural women to the city.

Krótke, Karole. "The Socio-Economic Evolution of the Inhabitants of a Desert City: The Case of Omdurman." In FROM MADINA TO METROPOLIS: HERITAGE AND CHANGE IN THE NEAR EASTERN CITY, edited by L. Carl Brown, pp. 150-65. Princeton, N.J.: Darwin Press, 1973.

Omdurman has attracted a heavy stream of female migrants. In fact, until the 1950s the largest number of newcomers were women. While the trend has reversed, this city has served as a refuge for widows and for women whose husbands have gone elsewhere to seek employment.

Lam, Timothy Thim-Fook. THE GROWTH OF THE CHINESE COMMUNITY AND URBANIZATION IN THE MALAY PENINSULA. Kuala Lumpur: University of Malaysia, Department of Geography, n.d. 56 p.

While in the Chinese population as a whole men outnumber women, in the urban areas there are significantly more females than males. This has been especially true since the beginning of the twentieth century. Generally, urban employment opportunities are more ample for women than for men. Older women and widows frequently settle in the cities upon retirement.

Little, Kenneth Lindsay. AFRICAN WOMEN IN TOWNS: AN ASPECT OF AFRICA'S SOCIAL REVOLUTION. London: Cambridge University Press, 1973. 242 p.

One of the most significant monographs in the field, this study indicates that, as urban migrants, women are more determined than their male counterparts. For women, migration to the cities is a positive act. A whole range of women, in various situations, view the process of urban migration as a chance for greater independence.

_____. URBANIZATION AS A SOCIAL PROCESS: AN ESSAY ON MOVEMENT AND CHANGE IN CONTEMPORARY AFRICA. London: Routledge and Kegan Paul, 1974. 153 p.

Intended as a general survey of the field, this study makes a number of statements about women and the process of urbanization in Africa. There are a number of different colonial policies towards the urban migration of women. In the Congo, the Belgians wanted to create a stable urban labor force and expected the urban Congolese to remain permanent urban dwellers. Therefore, men were encouraged to bring their wives into the cities. Other parts of Africa are influenced by other colonial attitudes. Generally, migration to cities has been viewed as very positive by women, even though male urban migrants may outnumber women by as much as six or seven times.

Mabogunje, Akin L. URBANIZATION IN NIGERIA. London: University of London Press, 1968. 353 p.

The author discusses the variations between Nigerian cities in terms of differing sex ratios. In Ibadan, for example, there is a preponderance of females, because the men constantly return to their tribal land. In Lagos and the other new cities, however, men appear in larger number than women. Within the Yoruba region a substantial number of the women migrants are employed or self-employed in trades and crafts, while in the northern, Islamic regions of Nigeria there are fewer opportunities for women.

McGee, T.G. "An Aspect of Urbanization in South-East Asia." In READINGS IN SOCIAL GEOGRAPHY, edited by Emrys Jones, pp. 224-39. London: Oxford University Press, 1975.

The author sets forth certain generalizations about rural-urban migration in Europe during the Industrial Revolution and then compares them with contemporary cityward migration in Southeast Asia. Among the comparisons he notes that Southeast Asian city migration has been more consistently male. This is partly explained in all the countries involved except for Cambodia and Indonesia, where the population as a whole is more thoroughly masculine than feminine. The author asserts that the Chinese communities are important since they have a large sex imbalance, with more men concentrated in urban areas. The general excess of urban men to women is most acute in the age bracket fifteen to fifty-nine and even more so in the fifteen to thirty-nine group. Only the Philippines are excepted here, where women clearly outnumber men, especially when looking at the ages fifteen to twenty-four. The author demonstrates that Philippine urban migration took a dramatic shift after 1948, when it became preponderantly female. The author concludes that Southeast Asia, like the Philippines, may eventually conform to the European Industrial Revolution model which is essentially heavily male in the earliest phase, equally balanced between men and women in the second, and heavily female in its third phase.

Mair, Lucy Philip. "African Marriage and Social Change." In SURVEY OF AFRICAN MARRIAGE AND FAMILY LIFE, edited by Arthur Phillips, pp. 1-159. London: Oxford University Press, 1953.

The author attributes the sex imbalance in African cities to the impossibility of African women joining their husbands in town. The conditions of African urban life are such that many men do not want to take their wives with them. In southern Africa where polygamy is not legally sanctioned there are a large number of prostitutes among the urban women. Central African cities see a substantial influx of young women at the age of marriage, because the rural areas have been depopulated of young men. This is a traditionally matrilineal region where much familial authority is wielded by one's mother's brother. This tradition has declined, however, with the flow of young men into the cities, where they are able to earn a living. Among the salient characteristics of West African cities are a fairly high divorce rate, due to the constant movement of women away from their husbands, either back to rural areas in order to fulfill kin obligations, or out on trading expeditions.

Martin, Harry W. "Correlates of Adjustment among American Indians in an Urban Environment." HUMAN ORGANIZATION 23 (Winter 1964): 290-95.

Navaho, Sioux, and Choctaw Indians are ranked from low to high in terms of degree of acculturation and assimilation. All three groups demonstrate adaptive behavior in cities, but differences among them are much more apparent among the women than among the men.

Mathewson, Marie Asnes. "Southern Ghanaian Women: Urban Residence and Migrational Cycles." Ph.D. Dissertation, University of Rochester, 1973.

This urban ethnography studies the social life of women, all of whom are migrants, living in Madina, a suburban development in Accra. The goal of the research is to determine the types of resources, institutions, and networks, both urban and nonurban, which these female migrants can use in the process of adjusting to city life. The research assumes that there is regularity and observable patterns in migrant women's methods of handling crises. This is a participant observation project, which includes informal interviews. The author concludes that the migrant women interact with each other in terms of shared values and expectations. As their urban residence gets longer they acquire a set of urban contacts who are or can be used in various problem situations. These same women also maintain contact and communication with people in home town communities, as well as kinspeople in other places. In certain types of crises, including childbirth, debt, severe illness, and divorce, these women tend to exploit their extra-urban contacts. This practice usually entails leaving the city. Therefore these women are involved in a regular migratory pattern, into and out of the city. The second part of the dissertation focuses on the migratory patterns of these women and presents a model based on quantitative data for 141 women. The model asserts that women will normally migrate into the city as dependents of husbands or some other men, whereas independent, female-headed migrations occur rarely.

Natal Regional Survey, University of Natal, Institute for Social Research. BAUMANNVILLE: A STUDY OF AN URBAN AFRICAN COMMUNITY. Cape Town: Oxford University Press, 1959. 79 p.

Published under the auspices of the Institute for Social Research of the University of Natal, this survey looks at an area north of the city of Durban. The building of this town signified the recognition by city officials that Africans were becoming permanent urbanites. The largest number of residents of Baumannville are Zulus, but women are more heavily concentrated among the Zulus than the men. According to the study this implies that male urban migrants can be drawn in from greater distances than women migrants. The community is preponderantly female, with women having a higher median age than the men (19.4 for the men as opposed to 20.7 for the women). The numerical superiority of women (about 85 men to every 100 women) is partly due to official policy which allows widows to stay on as household heads.

Oram, Nigel D. TOWNS IN AFRICA. London: Oxford University Press, 1965. 98 p.

Those cities which are now receiving the largest numbers of migrants tend to have a larger number of men than women. Of those women who migrate to cities, some are traders, while most cities of Central and East Africa provide very few employment opportunities for women.

Papaneck, Hanna. "Women in Cities: Problems and Perspectives." In WOMEN AND WORLD DEVELOPMENT, edited by Irene Tinker, Michele Bo Bromsen, and Mayra Buvinić, pp. 54-69. New York: Praeger Publishers, 1976.

The author identifies five problem areas for urban women: (1) the socioeconomic status of women, (2) women's geographic and social mobility, (3) women's work, (4) education and training of women, and (5) the power of women's groups and associations. The author maintains that cities are the belleweather of women's social change. Changes or problems in women's status in the cities indicate the trend for the whole of the society.

Paydarfar, A.A. "Modernization Process and Demographic Changes." SOCIOLOGICAL REVIEW 15 (July 1967): 141-53.

This article, based on data from ten countries as well as thirteen provinces of Iran, analyzes the indexes of industrialization, education, and urbanization. It then relates these factors to age-sex composition, marital status, occupational involvement, fertility level, and migration patterns.

Ross, Marc Howard. THE POLITICAL INTEGRATION OF URBAN SQUATTERS. Evanston, Ill.: Northwestern University Press, 1973. 228 p.

This study of Mathare, a squatter slum within the city of Nairobi, Kenya, indicates that while in the rest of Nairobi men outnumber women, in the squatter community the reverse is true; women outnumber men.

Rosser, Colin. URBANIZATION IN INDIA. New York: International Urbanization Survey, Ford Foundation, [1973?]. 106 p.

The author found a sex-selective pattern of urban migration in

India. The typical migrant is male. The fewest women are found in the largest cities. Strikingly absent are women in their child-bearing ages.

_____. URBANIZATION IN TROPICAL AFRICA: A DEMOGRAPHIC INTRO-DUCTION. New York: International Urbanization Survey, Ford Foundation, [1973?]. 74 p.

Throughout tropical Africa the author found a unifying demographic pattern. This pattern was characterized by the heavy number of men and the shortage of women in the urban population.

Saxena, Sudha. TRENDS OF URBANISATION IN UTTAR PRADESH. Agra, India: Satish Book Enterprise, 1970. 275 p.

Throughout Uttar Pradesh, urban men outnumber urban women. This is particularly striking in the larger city, where the scarcity of women is even more acute than in other cities. The author sees this as part of the transitory nature of much of the urban pop-ulations. Many urban dwellers in this region are only temporary migrants to the cities.

Sharma, J.C. "Sex Composition in the Urban Population in Rajasthan." GEOGRAPHICAL REVIEW OF INDIA 28 (September 1966): 1-17.

The urban demography of Rajasthan shows a striking disparity be-tween the number of men and women, yet of all Indian urban pop-ulation areas, this one has one of the lowest differences between urban and rural sex ratios. The author attributes this to three fac-tors: (1) biological factors, including the toll of women who die in childbirth; (2) social factors, including the system of purdah which the author assesses has had a very negative effect on the health of women; and (3) economic-industrial factors which have siphoned off men from the rural areas, and provided only limited employment opportunities for urban females.

Simmance, Alan J.F. URBANIZATION IN ZAMBIA. New York: Interna-tional Urbanization Survey, Ford Foundation, 1972. 52 p.

In Zambia there are more men than women, even though the fe-male urban population is growing at a much faster rate than the male urban population. The author asserts that this may be due to the movement of female dependents out of the villages, to the city to meet their husbands.

Van Allen, Judith. "African Women, 'Modernization,' and National Libera-tion." In WOMEN: A COMPARATIVE STUDY, edited by Lynne B. Iglitzen and Ruth Ross, pp. 25-46. Santa Barbara, Calif.: Clio Books, 1976.

Many urban African women are rural and urban at the same time.

Many spend up to half of the year in their village, while others will travel from the city to the village two times a year, in order to plant and to harvest. The urban surplus of men over women is slowly shrinking. The author uses the term "semi-male" to describe the typical African town. This means that there is a surplus of unmarried men, but the sex ratio is significantly less than five to one. In the towns considered, women are able to control and monopolize the marketplace. In terms of urban migration patterns, 75-80 percent of all urban African women have come to the cities with their husbands. Generally African men prefer to marry rural women rather than city women. An urban man may in fact live in town with a woman while he is saving his money in order to marry a village woman. Thus, most urban women will fall into one of two categories: either they are married and living with their husbands, or they are unmarried and unmarriageable.

Van der Horst, Sheila T. AFRICAN WORKERS IN TOWN: A STUDY OF LABOUR IN CAPE TOWN. Cape Town: Oxford University Press, 1964. 104 p.

There are strikingly few women in Cape Town. This is in part due to official government policy which sought to stem the growing tide of women into the city. Among male workers in Cape Town, the intention to remain a permanent urbanite is correlated positively with the proportion of those who have wives living with them.

Weintraub, Philipp. "Demographic Aspects of Rural-Urban Migration in European Countries since the Second World War." In CITY AND PEASANT: A STUDY IN SOCIOCULTURAL DYNAMICS, vol. 220, edited by Anthony L. La Ruffa, pp. 524-37. ANNALS OF THE NEW YORK ACADEMY OF SCIENCES. New York: New York Academy of Sciences, 1974.

There have been a wide variety of contemporary European migratory experiences. They differ from country to country. The process of sex selection varies with the nature of the migration. Rural-to-urban migrations tend to be short-distance, which tends to attract women. Women generally migrate short distances because in the cities they can avail themselves of opportunities for unskilled and service jobs more than men can. The only time when men are more attracted to short-distance, rural-to-urban migrations is when there has been a rapid expansion of industry. Then men outnumber women in the stream of migrants. A high proportion of the women migrants are single, while those families which elect to migrate tend to be smaller than those which remain in the rural areas. This is partly due to the youthfulness of the migrating women.

Youssef, Nadia H. "Women in Development: Urban Life and Labour." In WOMEN AND WORLD DEVELOPMENT, edited by Irene Tinker, Michele Bo

Bromsen, and Mayra Buvinic, pp. 70–77. New York: Praeger Publishers, 1976.

The author begins with some worldwide statistics on urban women. Women comprise 50 percent of all urban dwellers in South America, 40 percent in Asia, and 17 percent in Africa. The paper then develops a rationale for integrating women into the process of urban development, and points out how women can contribute to this process. The author lays out a number of negative effects that urbanization and modernization have on women's lives: (1) new methods of production and new technological developments tend to undermine women's economic independence; (2) modernization may increase sex role differences, thus enhancing male status, while lowering that of females. This gap in role and status becomes especially acute when women are not integrated into the process of technological change; (3) rapid urbanization, especially when it is the result of migration to cities, tends to produce a cycle of economic exploitations of women, among which the author includes prostitution and slum life. Much of the urban migrant stream is made up of unsupported females and their dependents. The author suggests a number of policy changes.

Section II

WOMEN IN URBAN FAMILIES

This section treats works dealing with the structure and composition of urban families and the particular roles of women within those families. Included are books and articles dealing with courtship, marriage, and sexual patterns, as well as extrafamilial sex patterns.

Anderson, Michael. FAMILY STRUCTURE IN NINETEENTH CENTURY LAN-CASHIRE. Cambridge: University Press, 1971. 230 p.

> In several specific chapters dealing with urban family life and family structure, the author notes that the dominant urban pattern was one where husband and wife had segregated conjugal roles. While the family as a whole was held together by bonds of affection, the strongest of these bonds was between the mother and her children. One important role of the urban mother was to protect her children from the father.

Anderson, Robert T., and Anderson, Gallatin. "Sexual Behavior and Urbanization in a Danish Village." SOUTHWESTERN JOURNAL OF ANTHROPOLOGY 16 (Spring 1960): 93–109.

> This study, based on ethnographic field work conducted during 1955–57, analyzes changing sexual behavior in a village which became a suburb of Copenhagen in the 1890s. Among the changes observed by the researchers were the following: (1) meetings between females and males changed from multi-age events in the village stage to single-age, youth events in the urban stage; (2) courtship and marriage changed from a serious and solemn engagement to a pattern of several engagements; (3) sexual intercourse changed from a privilege reserved for those who were ring-engaged to basically a series of sexual liaisons; finally, (4) the sanctions against promiscuity changed from the ostracism of village life for unwed mothers and promiscuous girls to a situation of greater tolerance, based partly on greater anonymity.

Bernard, Guy. "Conjugalité et le rôle de la femme." CANADIAN JOURNAL

OF AFRICAN STUDIES 6 (1972): 261-74.

This is an analysis of the effects of urbanization on middle-class male and female role patterns in Kinshasa. Only the male role is fully integrated into the urban environment. Women's roles retain their traditional core, although stripped of their economic and social functions which were based on the needs and demands of an agrarian society. An urban woman is generally better educated than her village counterpart, but her functional role is diminished in the city as she becomes increasingly subordinated to her more urbanized husband.

Bird, Mary. "Urbanisation, Family and Marriage in Western Nigeria." In her URBANIZATION IN AFRICAN SOCIAL CHANGE, pp. 59-74. Edinburgh: Centre of African Studies, 1963.

Under urban conditions a family pattern develops where loyalty is directed toward the conjugal unit, which is essentially isolated. The wife's reaction to this development is to seek a new type of joint conjugal role in the relationship with her husband. Her husband, however, who has a wider social sphere outside the home, is more interested in a segregated conjugal role relationship. This sex-linked discrepancy can lead to serious urban familial problems. This study, which is based on data from the 1952-53 Census, studies Nigeria Yoruba, a group which was traditionally urban in that it has long lived in towns. But with the development of cash economy, the author believes the group became "urbanized." Among the effects of urbanization on the family the author cites (1) the decline of polygamy, which in the city becomes an economic and social liability; (2) the separation of the conjugal unit from the lineage compound; and (3) a more intimate relationship between husband and wife, even though the sex segregation has become an important pattern.

Blood, Robert Oscar. "Impact of Urbanization on American Family Structure and Functioning." SOCIOLOGY AND SOCIAL RESEARCH 49 (October 1964): 5-16.

This study used information collected from a random sample of 178 women on the fringe of Detroit. The author asserts that urbanization has enabled families to assume new functions and to alter existing structures in order to accommodate a new division of labor. One form this accommodation takes is the growing equalization of roles between husband and wife. The significance of the impact of urban life on the family can be seen beyond the metropolitan area; the changing structure extends to adjacent farm families as well. Consequently, farm families and city families share many features.

Bott, Elizabeth. FAMILY AND SOCIAL NETWORK: ROLES, NORMS, AND

EXTERNAL RELATIONSHIPS IN ORDINARY URBAN FAMILIES. London: Tavistock, 1957. 252 p.

This study of twenty London families attempts to measure the degree of segregation between husbands and wives, in terms of both roles and relationships. The author concludes that the degree of segregation varies directly with the family's connections to outside social networks. The trend of urban family life is towards a change in families--away from forced female domesticity towards one of "joint" marital relationship, with the husband and wife in a companionate role. This trend therefore accounts for loose, external family ties.

_____. "Urban Families: Conjugal Roles and Social Networks." HUMAN RELATIONS 8 (1955): 345-84.

Based on a study of twenty families, this article attempts to interpret various urban patterns of husband-wife conjugal roles. At one end of the scale the researcher found a pattern of strict division of labor which was characterized by a segregated conjugal role relationship. At the other end was a pattern where behavior and activities were interchangeable. This pattern was identified as a joint conjugal role relationship.

Brandel, Mia. "Urban Lobola Attitudes: A Preliminary Report." AFRICAN STUDIES 17 (1958): 34-50.

Focusing on Johannesburg and a group of professional, educated women, the author discusses the urban lobola--matrimonial compensation. The author asserts that a change in status for these African women brings with it a change in the significance of the lobola in the city. The lobola is not dying out in the cities, despite the drift of many urban Africans towards European-style, Christian marriages. What has happened is that the lobola has shifted functions. It no longer has its primary function, the transferring of the status of the children of the union. In the city the lobola satisfies certain peculiarly urban needs. These changes reflect changes in the social structure and changes in kinship patterns. The author concludes that the maintenance of the lobola helps stabilize urban marriages and helps create a link of security for a daughter with her parental home. Many educated women in Johannesburg do indeed believe that their lobola signifies their social worth in the community.

Caldwell, John Charles. POPULATION GROWTH AND FAMILY CHANGE IN AFRICA: THE NEW URBAN ELITE IN GHANA. Canberra: Australian National University Press, 1968. 222 p.

Based on interviews and survey data, this study examined wives and husbands between the ages of eighteen and forty-four in 1963.

The author was interested in ascertaining popular attitudes towards reproductive behavior. As a result, the author uncovered data about family patterns generally. In the upper socioeconomic groups with male household heads, women tended to marry at a later age. Where husbands and wives talked to each other about family planning, there was a general social concern for the high national population trends. Most of the urban elite families were closer to Western families in style and attitude than to rural Ghanaian families. In these families there were few marked differences of opinion between the husband and wife. Especially among the women there was a growing concensus that a family of four children was large enough; these women knew a good deal about contraception, and practiced it.

Centro Latinamericano Demografia. "Population Policy and the Family: The Latin American Case." In THE POPULATION DEBATE: SYMPOSIUM ON POPULATION AND THE FAMILY, HONOLULU, 6-15 AUGUST, 1973, vol. 2, pp. 327-37. Santiago, Chile: CELADE, 1973.

In the urban Latin American context a number of different family types emerge: a working-class proletarian family and a marginal or subproletarian family. Among these marginal families there are a large number of consensual unions and female-based households. Many of these women are not eligible for social insurance or are not covered by various types of social legislation. Women in these families have a high rate of economic activity outside the home. Among the working-class families which have some economic stability, there is a fairly clear division of labor between the sexes. The father is the economic supporter while the mother is the family socializer, despite sporadic, part-time employment outside the home.

Church, Roy A. ECONOMIC AND SOCIAL CHANGE IN A MIDLAND TOWN: VICTORIAN NOTTINGHAM, 1815-1900. London: Frank Cass, 1966.

The author concludes that the high rate of infant mortality may have been due to infanticide. Large numbers of working mothers, migrants to the city, found the double burden of work and motherhood extremely difficult and resorted to infanticide, using such methods as starvation and drugs.

Clignet, Remi. "Environmental Change, Types of Descent and Child Rearing Practices." In THE CITY IN MODERN AFRICA, edited by Horace Miner, pp. 257-96. London: Frederick A. Praeger, 1967.

Using an ethnographic approach the author studies the Abure and Bete in Ivory Coast cities. He attempts to measure the impact of modernization and urbanization on marriage patterns and on the status of women within the domestic circle. This phenomenon varies according to traditional patterns and specific behavior. Differences between the Abure and the Bete women in employment, marriage patterns, education, and the like led the author to assert that the large category of "urban women" had to be broken down into more refined groups for study. The more urban and more modern families whom the author found among clerical workers tend to be more conservative in their family practices, demonstrating higher rates of polygamy than less urbanized manual workers. Similarly, child-rearing practices vary with the inconsistencies of women's status in the urban environment. To measure this the author considered fertility levels, pre- and perinatal rituals and practices, employment, weaning of children and modes of discipline, authority patterns within the family, and rates and styles of marriage.

———. MANY WIVES, MANY POWERS: AUTHORITY AND POWER IN POLYGYNOUS FAMILIES. Evanston, Ill.: Northwestern University Press, 1970. 380 p.

This monograph on polygyny treats the Ivory Coast and several tribes within it. For the Abure, urbanization brought with it greater integration, both social and economic, of women into the affinal group. Urban polygyny adds many new factors into the family structure because cowives in the city where plural marriage is in decline have less clearly defined social roles. The urban-rural contrast is particularly visible for the Abure. Urbanization has also changed patterns for recruiting both single spouses as well as cowives. The Bete were the other group under consideration. Among the Bete, relative power within the domestic unit of senior cowives is actually enhanced in the city because they are so scarce and because they are able to earn money in the urban economy, especially as traders in the market. However, single spouses gain even more in the cities. Generally, urbanization breaks down ethnic differences among women in their child-rearing techniques, in degree of dependence on husband, and in attitudes towards parental responsibilities.

———. "Urbanization and Family Structure in the Ivory Coast." COMPARATIVE STUDIES IN SOCIETY AND HISTORY 8 (July 1966): 385-401.

The author relates urbanization to changes in marriage and family. According to the author, urban women marry later than their rural counterparts and usually choose a mate from outside the ethnic group, have greater freedom in spending money, wean their children earlier, and exert greater influence and discipline over their children. Urbanized women in Africa also retain some characteristics which set them apart from Western urbanized women. Most important, urban African families have some degree of matrifocality. The increase of family functions for the urban African wife in part leads to greater autonomy and authority.

Comhaire, Jean L. "Some Aspects of Urbanization in the Belgian Congo." AMERICAN JOURNAL OF SOCIOLOGY 62 (July 1956): 8-13.

> While the urbanized masses in Leopoldville and Brazzaville are tribe-conscious and mix very little with members of other tribes, certain intertribal customs are developing. The dowry or bride-price is becoming a universal urban phenomenon, while in the tribal setting only some groups use this. Another shared characteristic is the growing importance of the father in the family.

Denich, Bette S. "Urbanization and Women's Roles in Yugoslavia." ANTHROPOLOGICAL QUARTERLY 49 (January 1976): 11-19.

> Under consideration here is the large-scale rural-to-urban migration within Yugoslavia, under the jurisdiction of a socialist government which rhetorically stresses sex equality. Rural peasant life is patrilocal, with the male head of the household in a clearly dominant position. In the rural setting a hierarchical sexual structure is reinforced by codes for behavior and elaborate sets of belief. The central question of the article is "what happens to people socialized under this type of culture when they are confronted with new conditions in urban society?" The author discusses the effects of employment on women's lives as well as the effects of the urban environment on the adaptation process which peasant women undergo. Generally, the author finds greater partnership between husbands and wives in urban households; although their roles are not equal, there is greater cooperation than before. Wives have a greater degree of autonomy because of the physical separation of their husbands' work from the home. This separation also leads to an increase in urban women's authority within the home, while public roles are left to men. This new household form has been effective in easing the transition from peasant to urban life. However, there is still sex role dichotomy in spite of official ideology.

Djamour, Judith. MALAY KINSHIP AND MARRIAGE IN SINGAPORE. London: Athlone Press, 1959. 151 p.

> Malayans in Singapore have a high rate of divorce and a generally unstable marital structure. In spite of a low level of female education in almost all aspects of household activity, wives assumed either an equal or a greater share of the authority than their husbands. With the increase of urban divorce, there has been pressure from women's groups to reform existing divorce laws. Usually a women's kin will support her. This allows women to opt out of unpleasant marriages. Women are almost always welcomed back by their mothers.

Dore, Ronald Philip. CITY LIFE IN JAPAN: A STUDY OF A TOKYO WARD. Berkeley and Los Angeles: University of California Press, 1958. 472 p.

This study of the Shitayama-Cho ward makes a number of points about urban Japanese women and their family lives. The author attempts to integrate material about employment of these women into a general picture of family structure.

Eames, Edwin. "Urban Migration and Joint Family in a North Indian Village." JOURNAL OF DEVELOPING AREAS 1 (January 1967): 163-78.

This study of Senapur asserts that certain aspects of urbanization may actually strengthen the traditional joint family. The movement of married men to the cities will reinforce village family ties by making the developing, urban nuclear families more dependent on the larger joint unit.

Einsiedel, Luz A. "Urbanization and the Filipino Home." HEMISPHERE (Australia) 7 (June 1963): 27-29.

This impressionistic study asserts that women have the major role in adjusting the family to urban life. This burden is particularly difficult for those urban women who must work outside the home. The author also presents a synopsis of a report by Community Development Research Council of the University of Philippines which studied urban families in the cities and suburbs of Marikena, Rizal Province.

Ferraro, Gary P. "Tradition of Transition: Rural and Urban Kinsmen in East Africa." URBAN ANTHROPOLOGY 2 (Fall 1973): 214-31.

Rural ties are maintained by Kikuyu migrant men in Nairobi partly because it is so expensive to maintain a wife and children in the city. Consequently, wives and children are left in the countryside. The author concludes there is little difference in the intensity of kinship ties among Kikuyu in Nairobi as compared to Kikuyu in the rural district.

Frazier, E. Franklin. "The Impact of Urban Civilization upon the Negro Family." AMERICAN SOCIOLOGICAL REVIEW 2 (October 1937): 609-18.

In this now classic and controversial essay, the author asserts that the maternal type family can offer no resistance to the disintegration of urban life. While a stable Negro family was in the process of evolving after slavery in the rural South, the northern, urban migration has undone the stability and has crumbled the structure of the Negro family. This is particularly devastating among the poor where there is a high rate of maternal employment, a staggering dependence on charity, increased delinquency among youth, and common unmarried motherhood. All of these characteristics are the result of urbanization.

_____ . "The Negro Family in Bahia, Brazil." AMERICAN SOCIOLOGICAL REVIEW 7 (August 1942): 465-78.

> Based on a study of fifty families, the author noted that racial mixture, which has been extensive in Brazil, has led to the disappearance of the African family structure. This has been accelerated by the breakdown of the rural patriarchy. Where Negro families have adopted an institutionalized family form, they have done so as a result of contact with Brazilian (or Portuguese) culture. This pattern will become more and more intense as Brazil becomes more urbanized; as a result Negroes will merge even more with the general population.

Gartley, Jaco E., and Belknap, Ivan. "Is a New Family Form Emerging in the Urban Fringe?" AMERICAN SOCIOLOGICAL REVIEW 18 (October 1953): 551-57.

> This study of suburbanization in the 1950s noted that in the suburban areas there has been a higher fertility rate than in the central city. Similarly, there have been more marriages occurring at a younger age. The researchers also noted that there has been an increase in female employment, for both single and married women. This has been particularly significant for the employment of married women with children aged twelve to seventeen. The authors attempt to generalize about the positive and integrative role of the family types developing in "suburbia."

Gerken, Egbert. "Social Structure and the Industrial Town: The Case of Social Change in Jinja and Busoga, Uganda." In THE INDUSTRIAL TOWN AS A FACTOR OF ECONOMIC DEVELOPMENT: THE EXAMPLE OF JINJA UGANDA, edited by Egbert Gerken, Hartmut Brandt, and Bernd Schubert, pp. 291-441. Munich: Weltforum Verlag, 1972.

> Among the number of observations offered here is that the decline in polygamy is not related to a change in values or norms concerning plural marriage, but that urban economic realities make polygyny difficult. Urban men may be seen as "monogamists against their will." With urbanization, there is also an increase in the age at which women marry. This is especially true among the more stabilized urbanites, rather than among the recent newcomers from the countryside. Among the most urbanized elements of the population there is a greater willingness to limit the number of children. The most critical variable seems to be the type of urban occupation of the husband/father. A larger proportion of urban women are interested in being employed outside the home than women in the rural areas. Similarly, urban women have a much larger scope of decision making than their rural counterparts. This is especially true for decisions about spending money for family consumption.

González, Nancy L. Solien. BLACK CARIB HOUSEHOLD STRUCTURE: A STUDY OF MIGRATION AND MODERNIZATION. Seattle: University of Washington Press, 1969. 163 p.

In Livingston, Guatemala, a consanguineal family system is developing among the females, who predominate in the urban migration. This system is based on the mother and her child/children. This family dyad, according to the author, is inextricably linked to the whole process of modernization and urbanization. It is particularly evident in societies where women outnumber men.

González, Nancy L. Solien, and Béhar, Moises. "Child Rearing Practices, Nutrition, and Health Status." MILBANK MEMORIAL FUND QUARTERLY 44 (April 1966): 77-96.

This study of urban migration in Brazil points out that with urbanization there is a decline in the age of weaning a child as well as a decline in the universality of breast feeding. This is partly due to patterns of urban female employment.

Gore, Madhave Sadashiv. "The Impact of Industrialization and Urbanization on the Aggrawal Family in the Delhi Area." Ph.D. Dissertation, Columbia University, 1961.

The author begins with a discussion of the traditional Aggrawal family structure (the business caste). That family structure, a joint system which is part of a peasant agricultural economy, is characterized by the subordination of women as a result of a pattern of eldest male authority. There is also a high degree of sex role segregation, based on the purdah system. The author attempts to measure changes in this traditional family structure among 400 Aggrawal. Urban women exhibit less conformity to the tradition than rural and urban families which are more typically nuclear rather than joint. The pattern of sex segregation especially undergoes changes in the urban environment. The nuclear family is unable to sustain a rigid system of purdah. The sample of urban women are usually more affluent than the sample of rural women and the author raises the possibility that the changes may reflect changes in economic status as well as changes based on urban residence. This dissertation was also reprinted as a monograph: URBANIZATION AND FAMILY CHANGE. Bombay: Popular Prakashan, 1968. 273 p.

Graves, Nancy Beatrice. "City, Country, and Child-Rearing: A Tricultural Study of Mother-Child Relationships in Varying Environments." Ph.D. Dissertation, University of Colorado, 1969.

This dissertation asks two questions: (1) what is the relationship between certain maternal attitudes of internal controls with respect to child rearing and future-oriented methods of child rearing;

(2) what are the effects of acculturation and urbanization on these
attitudes and methods. The study involved lower-income urban
and rural mothers of Spanish-American (United States) background
and Bagandas, from Uganda, East Africa. The methodology used
was a survey followed by open-ended interviews and systematic
observation with case studies. The conclusion answered the two
questions. First the author asserted that maternal attitudes based
on a high degree of internal control were directly related to more
frequent use of future-oriented teaching methods in both groups
under study. Secondly, the adjustment to urban life was related
to a number of detrimental changes in child-rearing practices,
which both groups underwent. The impact of social change through
urbanization was much greater and more intense for the Spanish
women who were also undergoing the process of acculturation.
This was not a factor for the women in the Uganda case, since
the urban move did not involve a move into another culture.

Gulati, Subhash Chander. "Impact of Literacy, Urbanization, and Sex Ratios
on Age at Marriage in India." ARTHA VIJÑANA 11 (December 1969):
685-97.

The author attempted to correlate overall levels of education, overall rates of urbanization, and sex ratios. He used a linear regression for each Indian state between explained variable and
explanatory variables, based on data from the 1961 Census. He
found that there was nowhere a negative linear association between urbanization and later age at marriage. The general spread
of education was a more conducive factor than urbanization in
the movement towards later marriage.

Gutkind, Peter Claus Wolfgang. "African Urban Family Life: Comments on
and Some Analysis of Some Rural-Urban Differences." CAHIERS D'ETUDES
AFRICAINES 3, no. 2 (1962): 149-217.

The author points out the interrelationship of African urbanism
and rural-urban fertility levels with certain characteristics of urban African marriage. Based on data gathered between 1956 and
1958, the researcher surveyed 200 African women, half of whom
were urban, the other half rural. He found that in terms of stability of noncasual monogamous marriages, age of entry into marriage, and the gap between dissolved marriages did not register
any significant differences between the rural and urban areas.
The article offers a general review of much of the literature on
urban African family life and concludes that the sharp differences
noted between city and countryside in Africa have been overem-
phasized. He believes that the standard rural-urban dichotomy
does not take into consideration other significant factors of social
dynamics. The only aspect of African family life where a clear
urban pattern has emerged is family size.

Halstrom, Engin Inel. "Changing Sex Roles in a Developing Country."
JOURNAL OF MARRIAGE AND THE FAMILY 35 (August 1973): 546-53.

This study is based on data from Turkey, and surveys groups of
families with different degrees of exposure to urban life styles.
Three groups of females on a rural-to-urban continuum were selected in order to probe family structure and family dynamics.
The author was particularly interested in the wife's perceptions
of her own role and her relationship to her husband. Upper middle-
class urban wives tended to be more active and more modern
than dictated by traditional Turkish norms. Those women who
had migrated to the city had evolved more autonomous patterns
than rural women.

Hammel, Eugene A. "The Family Cycle in a Coastal Peruvian Slum and
Village." AMERICAN ANTHROPOLOGIST 63 (October 1961): 989-1005.

The slum of Ica (population 33,000) is compared to the village of
San Juan Bautista (population 700). Young adults in both places
of residence see the independent nuclear family as the ideal, but
young families in the urban slum do in fact set up such families
at a much earlier point. This is due to the absence of a stable,
self-sufficient kinship network of economic support. This makes
coresidence of spouse a crucial factor in economic survival of a
woman with young children. The slum area showed a high degree
of desertion, with many young women moving back and forth from
spouseless to coresident status. The matricenteredness of these
households is a function of greater male mobility in the slums.
The mother-child/children unit then becomes the most important
solidarity group. The author found in the urban slum a high degree of sibling solidarity, but noted that sympathy between women
will occasionally override sibling loyalty.

Harblin, Thomas Devaney. "Urbanization, Industrialization and Low-Income
Family Organization in Sao Paulo, Brazil." Ph.D. Dissertation, Cornell
University, 1971.

Intended as an exploratory study of the impact of urban life on
low-income couples and their attempts to cope with urbanization
and industrialization, this study focuses on Sao Paulo, Brazil. The
people studied fall into four categories: (1) rural natives, (2) recent
migrants to the city, (3) intermediate migrants, and (4) urban natives
(paulistanos). These four groups are compared in terms of changing
patterns of family responsibility and decision making within the
family. Generally, the urban family has a larger function because it must take on many of the tasks previously performed by
kinship groups and the corporate community in the rural setting.

Therefore, migrant families are forced to reorganize traditional patterns, many of which were based on sex-role segregation. The study asks if there was a patterned sequence to family reorganization and whether such factors as spouse's length of urban residence, occupational linkages, socioeconomic status, woman's status, and stages in the family life cycle affected the path of reorganization. This was analyzed with a purposive quota sample with comprehensive separate husband and wife interviews. The conclusion reached by the researcher was that among the studied couples, urbanization and industrialization have independent and complementary effects upon patterns of instrumental responsibility. Couples' experience with or exposure to urbanization eliminates the husband's dominance of tasks, while occupational linkages in the industrial world and economic independence calls upon women to show their competence and to assume a portion of responsibility for family financial matters and matters affecting the children. Wives gain responsibility for tasks, a condition which then creates opportunities for increased socialization to urban-industrial realities. The second area of increased wife responsibility is in determining the role of children. The most difficult accomplishment for wives is to share control of resources. The urban shift therefore means a shift to a pattern of increased female competence and responsibility. Among urban native couples there is even a pattern of wife dominance.

Harries-Jones, Peter. "Marital Disputes and the Process of Conciliation in a Copperbelt Town." RHODES-LIVINGSTON JOURNAL 35 (June 1964): 29-72.

According to this study of northern Rhodesian town life, focusing on the town of Roan, the economic conditions of urban life have changed the typical patterns of husband-wife relations. The major thrust of the change is that wives have an enlarged number of economic demands and that the family structure has not yet come to grips with these urban-economic changes. The author buttresses these generalizations with a number of cases which demonstrate the types of marital complaints brought to the Roan Township Citizens' Advice Bureau.

Hauser, Philip Morris. HANDBOOK FOR SOCIAL RESEARCH IN URBAN AREAS. Paris: UNESCO, 1965. 214 p.

The author makes a number of generalizations about the impact of urbanization on family life. He asserts that city life breaks down the traditional family, causing an increase in separations and divorces. Prostitution is also linked to the process of urbanization and is a widespread phenomenon in cities in developing areas. It is caused in part by the masculine nature of the population and the economic hardships encountered by women who are living through the transition from a subsistence to a cash economy.

Holleman, J.F. "The Changing Roles of African Women." In AFRICA IN TRANSITION, edited by Prudence Smith, pp. 71-78. London: Max Reinhardt, 1958.

According to this study the most unhappy urban women are the wives of upper-middle and professional-class families. This includes the wives of teachers, clerks, and ministers. The reason for their unhappiness with urban life is the isolation of the woman's wifely role from the other roles which rural women play. In rural areas women are integrated into a network of social relations based on kinship. In the amorphousness of urban life, women's social relationships are grounded in only one kinship relationship--with their husband. That is precisely the weakest relationship. The women included in this study of urban southern Rhodesia attribute their unhappiness and weak social position to the breakdown of the institution of the bridewealth (lobola).

Humphrey, Norma Daymond. "The Changing Structure of the Detroit Mexican Family: An Index of Acculturation." AMERICAN SOCIOLOGICAL REVIEW 9 (December 1944): 622-26.

The traditional Mexican peasant family is patriarchal and extended; sons control their sister's activities and behavior. With movement to the city, the decline in the father's status has been gradual, so that overt conflict is avoided. There is a change in the father's role of exercising moral protection over his wife and his female children. This is partly because of the wife's increasing role in protection of the girls. The author asserts that in Detroit the men use their protective function as a way to prevent their wives from Americanizing. A small proportion of the Mexican women in Detroit have taken advantage of the freedom afforded them in the urban environment. This seems to be particularly true where the wife is significantly younger than her husband. The main generalization here is that women have retained their previous role status through the retention of Mexican culture and cultural values. In a significant number of cases, however, they have come to occupy a superordinated social position.

Humphreys, Alexander Jeremiah. NEW DUBLINERS: URBANIZATION AND THE IRISH FAMILY. London: Routledge, 1966. 295 p.

According to this study, the urban wife has assumed increasing responsibilities in both the economic and noneconomic sectors. One of the most significant effects of urbanization has been the greater authority which urban mothers must and do exercise over

all children, males as well as females. This seems to have produced a measurable anxiety over the raising of sons--an area in
Irish culture traditionally reserved for fathers. In spite of the
increase in the domestic responsibilities for Dublin wives, they
have not experienced any real rise in status. In the economic
sector, the author ascertains that Dublin girls, across class lines,
have attempted to gain access to traditionally male jobs. They
all seem to try to prolong their years in the labor force and generally denigrate the prospects of marriage. Finally, the author
notes that out of a frustration with urban life and its failure to
reward the wife's role, younger wives who have spent considerable
time in the labor force are demanding greater social and recreational equality with their husbands.

Izzett, Alison. "Family Life among the Yoruba in Lagos, Nigeria." In SO-
CIAL CHANGE IN MODERN AFRICA: STUDIES PRESENTED AT THE FIRST
INTERNATIONAL AFRICAN SEMINAR, MAKERERE COLLEGE, KAMPALA,
JANUARY, 1959, edited by Aiden W. Southall, pp. 305-15. London:
Oxford University Press, 1961.

The author concludes that many Yoruba marriages in Lagos fail.
A major cause of this instability in urban marriage is that the
wife will leave her husband as soon as he can no longer support
her. Parents have frequently sold their daughters into marriages
in the city because of their own economic problems and the
shakiness of their own family life. The author asserts that among
the Lagos Yoruba there is a wide variation in family structure.

Jahoda, Gustav. "Love, Marriage, and Social Change: Letters to the Advice Column of a West African Newspaper." AFRICA 29 (April 1959):
177-89.

According to this study, geographic mobility and urban life have
widened the circle of association for potentially meeting members
of the opposite sex. Persons then thrown back on their own resources for establishing meaningful relationships are frequently
confused in the environment of the city. Relationships frequently
develop across tribal lines, as well as across social and economic
barriers. These urban relationships and proposed marriages can
lead to family friction.

Janisch, Miriam. "Some Administrative Aspects of Native Marriage Problems
in an Urban Area." BANTU STUDIES 15 (March 1941): 1-12.

With urbanization and many of the disorganizing factors of city
life there is an absence of marriage registration. This leads to a
breakdown of many of the protections on family stability. A case
in point is the breakdown of the protective purposes of the lobola
because of its monetization. Similarly, urban living conditions
have been a factor in the deterioration of the mother-in-law or

father-in-law avoidance tradition. Most of the article is descriptive and is focused on the legal and administrative ramifications of urban African family life.

Kay, Paul. "Urbanization in the Tahitian Household." In PACIFIC PORT TOWNS AND CITIES: A SYMPOSIUM, edited by Alexander Spoher, pp. 63-73. Honolulu: Bishop Museum Press, 1963.

This study of a Papeete neighborhood, Manuhol, is a contrast between an urban area and a rural district in the island of Tahiti, Mahaena. In the urban neighborhood, families are more matrilocal and significantly more female centered. The city has a preponderance of women while the rural area has a surplus of men. Urban men have a higher rate of residential mobility than do urban women. There is a general disorganization of these urban households.

Kemper, Robert V. "Family and Household Organization among Tzintzuntzan Migrants in Mexico City." In LATIN AMERICAN URBAN RESEARCH: ANTHROPOLOGICAL PERSPECTIVES ON LATIN AMERICAN URBANIZATION, vol. 4, edited by Wayne A. Cornelius and Felicity Trueblood, pp. 23-45. Beverly Hills, Calif.: Sage Publications, 1974.

Among the peasant migrants under analysis here, the author found very few matrifocal families. This virtual absence of mother-centered families is attributed to the steady rates of male employment which allow the continuation of bilateral conjugal households. According to the findings, the quality of the husband-wife relationship is markedly affected by urbanization. The relationship in fact improves under urban conditions as the husband sheds much of the veneer of machismo and as the woman reinterprets the role of the "madre abnegada." The family is further democratized by the absence of the husband's mother. The author concludes that in this case urbanization has been an integrating rather than a disorganizing force. See also Kemper, Robert V., MIGRATION AND ADAPTATION: TZINTZUNTZAN PEASANTS IN MEXICO CITY. Beverly Hills, Calif.: Sage Publications, 1977. 224 p.

Kennedy, Beth C. "Rural-Urban Contrasts in Parent-Child Relationships in India." INDIAN JOURNAL OF SOCIAL WORK 15 (December 1954): 162-74.

The author compares an agricultural rural village, Kunigal, with Binnypet, a textile town in Bangalore. The author found that rural mothers placed much emphasis on building the character of the child, and emphasized helpfulness and affection. Rural women tolerated beatings by their husbands. The urban women had greater equality within the family and as a result demonstrated greater self-confidence. Women in the city expressed open anger when they felt mistreated by their husbands, and they expected their husbands to "spoil" the children. Female children were valued and were not treated significantly different than male children. The author generalized that in the industrial-urban community greater respect was shown for women than in the village setting, and that there was greater appreciation for the woman's role.

Keyfitz, Nathan. "A Factorial Arrangement of Comparisons of Family Size." AMERICAN JOURNAL OF SOCIOLOGY 58 (March 1953): 470-80.

This article is an example of the use of experimental design to study the interrelation of age at marriage, ethnicity, income level, education, and distance from city on fertility. Using census enumeration data, the central question then was whether farm families are smaller where residence is closer to large cities. The author found that distance from the city was in fact a significant factor in reducing family size. The generalization derived from the data was that cities had an impact on fertility beyond the immediate boundaries of the Standard Metropolitan Statistical Area.

Khalaf, Samir. PROSTITUTION IN A CHANGING SOCIETY: A SOCIO-LOGICAL SURVEY OF LEGAL PROSTITUTION IN BEIRUT. Beirut: Khayats, 1965. 163 p.

Prostitution is an urban phenomenon. Most of the prostitutes in the study were urban-born (73 percent), indicating that most of the women were not naive farm girls, preyed upon by the negative influences of city life. Most of the women studied had a high degree of physical mobility and the author saw this as evidence of the urban influences on the prostitutes. The study was based on a sample of 130 prostitutes, 64 first-class and 66 second-class prostitutes. The women were all interviewed by the researcher.

Khuri, Fuad Ishag al-. FROM VILLAGE TO SUBURB: ORDER AND CHANGE IN GREATER BEIRUT. Chicago: University of Chicago Press, 1975. 272 p.

This is a study of Chiya, an area which became suburbanized in the late 1950s. Marriage patterns in this suburb vary with section, and Muslims and Christians have different patterns of marriage, divorce, and remarriage. The author found only a slight degree of difference between natives and migrants of the same religion from rural areas, in terms of marriage and polygamy. Generally, migration to the suburb has done little to alter family patterns.

Korson, J. Henry. "Dower and Social Class in an Urban Muslim Community." JOURNAL OF MARRIAGE AND THE FAMILY 29 (August 1967): 527-33.

This study of the mehr (dower) in Karachi, Pakistan, surveyed 1,333 marriages, from three distinct socioeconomic groups: upper, middle, and lower class. The data suggested that urbanism has not made a difference in this institution and that the mehr serves as a form of economic security for the wife in the event of divorce or separation.

Krige, Eileen Jensen. "Changing Conditions in Marital Relations and Paternal Duties among Urbanised Natives." AFRICA 9 (January 1936): 1-23.

With only some statistical data, the article is largely descriptive. It studies three contiguous native urban areas within Pretoria, which together contain about 10,000 residents. Of these, half (50.6 percent) were either born in the city or were long-time city residents. Another 28.4 percent had lived in the city at least ten years or more. The author noted that even the urban-born natives and the long-time urbanites maintained rural, tribal ties. From the case studies included here, a number of generalizations were drawn. There was a high rate of illegitimacy which the author attributed to the breakdown of traditional controls on girls' activities. Less important was the disappearance of tribal censures on boys. In the city, the only deterrent to promiscuity was parental control, but that had eroded in the face of urban conditions. The author also discussed the changes in the nature of the lobola. In the city it had become commercialized and money was used instead of cattle as had been common in the rural areas. The author also pinpointed the urban causes of marital instability. Here she felt that the movement of women out of the city and back to the country, especially upon childbirth, created long periods of family separation. There are also high rates of male desertion which is linked in part to the failure of the lobola in the city. Finally, the breakdown in polygamy is discussed in terms of its impracticality in the urban environment. Other rural marriage customs, like the levirate, do persist without real change.

Kurian, George. THE INDIAN FAMILY IN TRANSITION: A CASE STUDY OF KERALA SYRIAN CHRISTIANS. Gravenhage: Mouton, 1961. 139 p.

Education has diminished previously sharp rural-urban differences in family structure. Urban contacts for previously isolated rural dwellers have widened horizons and weakened the position of the father as the religious and authoritative figure. Generally, the trend seems to be towards rural and urban agreement over family values, in favor of the urban model. A majority of those surveyed no longer believed in the tradition of keeping women in the home. There was also positive feeling about democratizing the family and diminishing the dominance of the father. The author did find some lag in the countryside in terms of attitudes toward dowries and the proper role of women.

Laidler, Percy Ward. "Native (Bantu) Beliefs Concerning Pregnancy and

Childbirth, Their Effects on Public Health Administration, and the Effects of Detribalisation or Urbanisation upon Infant Mortality Rates." SOUTH AFRICAN JOURNAL OF SCIENCE 38 (1931): 418-22.

> The study lays out first Bantu midwifery practices and discusses pre-, peri-, and postnatal Bantu customs in the traditional setting. There is a clear clash between these customs and the conditions of urban life. The author asserts that among the Bantu the age of menarche is lower among urban girls than rural girls, although no explanation is offered to explain the phenomenon. The author notes that chastity is rare among urbanized Bantu girls.

Lammermeier, Paul J. "The Urban Black Family of the Nineteenth Century: A Study of Black Family Structure in the Ohio Valley, 1850-1880." JOURNAL OF MARRIAGE AND THE FAMILY 35 (August 1973): 440-56.

> The urban black family in the nineteenth century was basically a two-parent, male-headed family which did not retain the characteristics of the slave family. Despite increasing residential segregation the only significant lessening of the two-parent, patrilocal family can be seen in proportion to the female-headed extended families.

Legerman, Caroline J. "Haitian Peasant, Plantation, and Urban Lower Class Family and Kinship Organization: Observation and Comments." In PAPERS OF THE CONFERENCE ON RESEARCH AND RESOURCES OF HAITI, edited by Richard P. Schaedel, pp. 71-84. New York: Research Institute for the Study of Man, 1969.

> This study of family and kinship compares rural peasants, residents of a large-scale commercial area, and an urban lower class. The research for this project was carried on during 1964-65. The urban area was characterized by unstable marriages and disorganized mating patterns. Many of the women were either professional or semiprofessional prostitutes. For urban women, employment opportunities reduced their dependence on men. Generally, the chances for earning a living for lower-class women were greater than for their male counterparts. The author asserts that the matricentric family which is common among lower-class Haitians is not an African inheritance but the result of socioeconomic factors, among them urbanization. This article can also be found in THE HAITIAN POTENTIAL: RESEARCH AND RESOURCES OF HAITI, edited by Vera Rubin and Richard P. Schaedel, pp. 17-22. New York: Columbia University, Teachers College Press, 1975.

Lehmann, Dorothea A. "African Urban Marriage in Northern Rhodesia." AFRICAN WOMEN 5 (December 1952): 14-16.

> Despite the high value placed on the independence of the individual in the urban setting, when it comes to marriage, women

are still viewed as legal minors and as dependent on others for consent. One of the changes due to the adjustment to urban life is that prenuptial negotiations are conducted by a few individuals rather than by two whole families. Polygamy is breaking down in the cities because it does not fit into the physical structure of urban households. More and more urban women are taking advantage of clinics for childbirth rather than going home to their tribal village.

Levine, Robert A. "Sex Roles and Economic Change in Africa." ETHNOLOGY 5 (April 1966): 186-93.

This article, based on qualitative observation rather than quantitative data, reports on a number of African societies. All of the societies under examination maintain a traditional ideal of male supremacy within the conjugal relationship. In East Africa and South Africa the form that labor migrations into the city has taken allows for continued husband dominance in family affairs. This cultural maintenance has occurred at the same time that the level of the wife's work has increased. This seems to have produced an irritability in women, which manifests itself in punitive behavior towards their children. In Nigeria, however, urbanization has increased and augmented women's traditional marketing roles, resulting in greater independence from their husbands. This has seriously strained and tested the ideal of male dominance. Men subsequently feel personally inadequate, and experience a sense of relative deprivation which they demonstrate by hostility towards women.

Levine, Robert A.; Klein, Nancy H.; and Owens, Constance R. "Father-Child Relationships and Changing Life-Styles in Ibadan, Nigeria." In THE CITY IN MODERN AFRICA, edited by Horace Miner, pp. 215-55. New York: Frederick Praeger, 1967.

This study asserts that under the pressures of urbanization and urban life the social distances between husband and wife have been limited. This has made the relationship more egalitarian and has lessened the previously dominant role of the man.

Lewis, Oscar. "The Culture of the Vecindad in Mexico City." In ACTAS DEL XXXIII CONGRESO INTERNACIONAL DE AMERICANISTAS: JULY 20-27, 1958, SAN JOSE, pp. 387-402. Reprinted in his ANTHROPOLOGICAL ESSAYS, pp. 427-40. New York: Random House, 1970.

This is a study of two neighborhoods in Mexico City inhabited primarily by poor rural migrants. Despite the cultural value of machismo, there has been a marked tendency towards the matri-centric family. This is caused in part by the frequency of male desertion. Women in the city have a very difficult time fulfilling their economic role.

_____. "Urbanization without Breakdown: A Case Study." SCIENTIFIC MONTHLY 75 (July 1952): 31-41.

This is a follow-up study of the author's research on the Tepotzlan village. This article follows 100 migrants from Tepotzlan into Mexico City where the author found little evidence of family breakup and male desertion. There were very few abandoned women and children.

Little, Kenneth Lindsay, and Price, Anne. "Some Trends in Modern Marriage among West Africans." AFRICA 37 (October 1967): 407-24.

Among modern, urban Africans there is a strong desire for companionate marriages along Western lines. This is especially true among educated and younger Africans. The article attempts to explain the motivation for the desire for monogamous marriage. The authors imply, but do not specifically discuss, an urban dimension to this move towards westernized marriages. The authors also note that extramarital sexual contacts for men are facilitated in the cities by the presence of significant numbers of prostitutes of various kinds. Urbanization, they assert, has put greater distance between individuals and their kin. This has been an important factor in the development of companionate type marriages.

Liu, William T.; Rubel, Arthur J.; and Yu, Elena. "The Urban Family of Cebu: A Profile Analysis." JOURNAL OF MARRIAGE AND THE FAMILY 31 (May 1969): 393-409.

This study of Cebu City, Philippines, surveyed 1,521 families. The wife in each family had at least five years urban residence, was below the age of forty-five, and had had at least one pregnancy. The data indicates that in the urban environment the sex-segregated society (barkada) continues and men generally resist the development of increased conjugal affectivity. There is some increase in male participation in the household which gives the wife a greater voice and power in family decisions and activities.

Lopata, Helena Z. "Social Relations of Widows in Urbanizing Societies." SOCIOLOGICAL QUARTERLY 13 (Spring 1972): 259-71.

Based on both primary and secondary analyses of the life styles of widows age sixty-five and over in rapidly urbanizing societies, this study asserts that the changes brought about by urbanization have a more profound effect on widows than on married women. The author discusses the impact of widowhood in a range of societies, covering a spectrum of urbanization. Included are the isolated farm, the village, the small town, small city, "urban village," ethnic community, self-selected homogeneous community, heterogeneous community, and the metropolitan complex.

_____. WIDOWHOOD IN AN AMERICAN CITY. Cambridge, Mass.: Schenkman, 1973. 369 p.

This monograph deals with widows in Chicago over the age of fifty. The author depicts a number of different types of urban widows: the self-initiating woman, those widows in ethnic communities whose lives within the city duplicate village patterns, and the social isolate. The urban component is critical to the analysis of the various reactions and responses to widowhood. The author asserts that the way different types of women readjust to society following the death of the husband is related to their location in the process of modernization. The widows observed resemble more closely widows in other cities than widows in small towns and rural areas. Finally, the author generalizes that urban life demands voluntaristic involvement which in turns depends on personally developed and initiated habits and attitudes.

Lupri, Eugen. "Contemporary Authority Patterns in the West German Family: A Study in Cross-National Validation." JOURNAL OF MARRIAGE AND THE FAMILY 31 (February 1969): 134-44.

The author tests the thesis that family decision-making power stems from economic resources, especially those economic resources which individuals bring with them into a marriage. One important variable in this model is employment of the wife, which is important for both urban and rural women. The urban-rural differences, therefore, are minimized. The study was based on 812 farm families and 514 urban families.

McLaughlin, Virginia Yans. "Like the Fingers of the Hand: The Family and Community Life of First-Generation Italian-Americans in Buffalo, New York, 1880-1930." Ph.D. Dissertation, State University of New York--Buffalo, 1970.

The author notes that the Italian peasant family remained strikingly stable after immigration and urbanization, rather than experiencing a process of disruption. There were very low levels of family disorganization and very little in the way of family change. Charity workers and welfare officials found very little male desertion of the family; few female-dominated, matriarchal households; low rates of illegitimacy; very little intergenerational conflict; and very little exogamous marriage. This stability remained despite high levels of male unemployment and the new work conditions produced by an industrial and urban society. Urbanization brought about no critical restructuring of family roles. This stability was due in part to the type of city under consideration; there were few employment opportunities open to unskilled females in Buffalo. In cities where more opportunities existed, female options would have expanded and there might have been some change. This would have been particularly challenging had the levels of

male unemployment been as high as in Buffalo. This dissertation
was distilled into article form and can be found as "Patterns of
Work and Family Organization: Buffalo's Italians." JOURNAL
OF INTERDISCIPLINARY HISTORY 2 (Autumn 1971): 299-314.

Marris, Peter. AFRICAN CITY LIFE. Kampala, Uganda: Transition Books,
1968. 261 p.

This study of Lagos, Nigeria, contrasts the role of women in traditional society with women in the urban environment. One area
under study was marriage. Because of urban property holdings
and patterns of wealth, greater emphasis has been placed on economic opportunities for women, especially in trading. The author
notes that in the city there has been a shift in emphasis from
male-derived relationships to female-derived relationships. One
particularly important area has been that of employment of married women. The high degree of their employment in the city is
correlated to the shakiness of marriage, as a guarantee of economic survival. Women seek to expand their economic options
in the city as they realize that marriage does not bring with it
a certainty of continued income. Employment for married women
is a form of insurance against marital breakup. Traditionally,
women had a subordinated status within the protection of the family into which they had married. Urban women on the other
hand were seen as more independent, even though this was at the
expense of their traditional protection. Finally, the author notes
that the economic realities of urban life have led to a decline
in the attractiveness of polygamy.

_____. FAMILY AND SOCIAL CHANGE IN AN AFRICAN CITY: A STUDY
OF REHOUSING IN LAGOS. Evanston, Ill.: Northwestern University Press,
1962. 180 p.

This is a study of family life in Lagos, Nigeria. The research
involves Yoruba, large numbers of whom are Muslims. Based
on four sets of interviews, the research was conducted between
1958 and 1959. Traditionally, the Yoruba have been town dwellers.
Women marry into their husband's family and live within his lineage
compound. Marriage does not deprive a woman of her rights and
responsibilities within her own family. In Lagos the household
has replaced the compound as the chief residential unit. These
households are not isolated from each other and brothers and sis-
ters are bound to each other through their mother. Polygamy is
common. Of the Muslims studied, half had more than one wife.
There was also a high rate of divorce in Lagos. In Lagos women
have less protection than in the traditional setting if something
happens to her husband--either death or divorce. Therefore she
needs greater personal independence, especially in economic
terms. Nine out of ten wives surveyed worked and used their
income for themselves and their children, as well as for their

kin. Husband and wife do not spend a great deal of time together. Generally the dispersal of the larger family group has
not been compensated for by more intense bonds of marriage. In
1955 there was a massive slum clearance project and the creation
of a rehousing estate. Here the isolation of households was much
greater. Household expenses were also greater. This caused
greater friction and disharmony between husband and wife since
the new pattern could not support the old way which allowed
greater independence to married women. Only those families
which were financially secure were able to make the transition
easily.

_____. "Slum Clearance and Family Life in Lagos." HUMAN ORGANIZA-
TION 19 (Fall 1960): 123-28.

The author describes the social life of a central Lagos slum. He
is particularly interested in the role of women in the economic
sphere and the concept of the woman's place in marriage. At
the rehousing estate fewer wives were able to earn money, since
the area was not conducive to trading, while those who continued
to trade were earning much less than before. At the same time
it was much more expensive to live in the suburban estate. Young
families had much more privacy on the estate and greater independence since there were fewer kin in the immediate area. Yet
the suburban relocation setting disrupted previously stable families. Families were frequently unable to support themselves because they no longer had the wife's income. Thus many wives
and children were sent back to the tribal village. Another op-
tion taken by some women was to return to the central city on
their own. Therefore there was a higher divorce rate in the
estate than in the central city. The author concludes with a
number of policy statements derived from the research.

Masuoka, Jitsuichi. "Urbanization and the Family in Japan." SOCIOLOGY
AND SOCIAL RESEARCH 32 (September-October 1947): 535-39.

This statistical analysis of Japanese family patterns attempts to
prove that urbanization has simplified the structure of the traditional family and has secularized it. The author concludes that
the family has in fact diminished and there has been a large increase in the number of late marriages.

Mathewson, J. Edward. "Impact of Urbanization on 'Lobola.'" JOURNAL
OF RACIAL AFFAIRS 10 (April 1959): 72-76.

The author describes the traditional lobola--an exchange of cattle
for the bride, representing purchase of the bride's childbearing
potential. The author then asks what changes occur in this practice with urbanization. Focusing on Benoni tribesmen of South
Africa who have moved to a city of over 90,000, it is noted

that in traditional rural society the lobola helped reduce premarital sex. In the city, with its peculiar economic pressures, the lobola has been so modified as to have lost this function. This article is journalistic and nonquantitative.

Meillassoux, Claude. URBANIZATION OF AN AFRICAN COMMUNITY: VOLUNTARY ASSOCIATIONS IN BAMAKO. Seattle: University of Washington Press, 1968. 165 p.

This descriptive study of Bamako, Mali, is based on research gathered between 1962 and 1963. Its main focus is the popular culture of the city, and in particular an urban club. The author asserts that urbanization and modernization have led to the rapid emancipation of women. In terms of economics, since urban married women are unable to make money selling their husband's produce, they are forced into greater independence. This in turn leads to the founding of women's mutual aid societies.

Mills, A.R. "Biological Aspects of the African Family in Sierra Leone." In URBANIZATION IN AFRICAN SOCIAL CHANGE, pp. 85-89. Edinburgh: University of Edinburgh Centre of African Studies, 1963.

A number of generalizations are made. The author notes that females have more choices for marriage in town. Urban men will marry later and there are fewer men who practice polygamy in the city. There are similarly fewer births in town, and family size is lower in town than in villages.

Modell, John, and Hareven, Tamara K. "Urbanization and the Malleable Household: An Examination of Boarding and Lodging in American Families." JOURNAL OF MARRIAGE AND THE FAMILY 35 (August 1973): 467-79.

The practice of taking in lodgers and boarders was so widespread in American cities that it constituted an institution by which the family came to terms with urban life. This practice provided income for women within the home. It also provided widows and single women over forty with an opportunity to set up their own urban households rather than having to live with their families.

Mogey, John M. FAMILY AND NEIGHBOURHOOD: TWO STUDIES IN OXFORD. London: Oxford University Press, 1956. 181 p.

This is the study of two neighborhoods: St. Ebbe's, a neighborhood-centered community, and Barton, a family-centered housing estate. In Barton there are fewer families where the husband and wife show real disagreement. In this estate there are more households where both husband and wife share domestic tasks. Only one-fourth of the families have rigid separation of tasks while at St. Ebbe's, two-thirds do. St. Ebbes' families are more supportive of wives' employment outside of the home than are residents of Barton.

Mukerji, Dhurjati Prasad. "Indian Women and the Modern Family." In STATUS OF WOMEN IN SOUTH ASIA, edited by Angadipuram Appadorai, pp. 65-73. Bombay: Orient Longmans, 1954.

This essay appears in a volume published under the joint auspices of UNESCO and the Asia Relations Organization, and contains the proceedings of a conference held in New Delhi, December 1952 to January 1953. According to the author there are a number of sociocultural factors which influence the status of women in India. Since urban, middle-class Indian women are expected to supplement the family income, there is a greater investment in their education. The author asserts that urban migration has done for women what all the reformist activity could never accomplish. However, Indian urban women face a number of problems. They receive very low pay for their work. They also have the double burden of work and domestic responsibilities. The author believes that urban women seek release from these problems through mass culture. The author also notes that urban women have experienced a decline in health.

Natal Regional Survey, University of Natal, Institute for Social Research. BAUMANNVILLE: A STUDY OF AN URBAN AFRICAN COMMUNITY. London: Oxford University Press, 1959. 79 p.

Published for the Institute for Social Research, this study views an urban community north of the city of Durban. The basic form of marriage here is monogamous Christian. This is due partly to official sanction and partly to the increased economic power of women. Marriage is quite expensive in the urban context. The lobola has persisted but the amount of money involved has gone up steadily since 1930. Recently there has been a trend towards later age at marriage, but opposition towards birth control persists. One area of change is in childbirth practices. Traditional patterns with a midwife are eroding in favor of hospitalization in modern facilities.

Ogburn, William F., and Nimkoff, Meyer F. TECHNOLOGY AND THE CHANGING FAMILY. Boston: Houghton Mifflin, 1955. 329 p.

The authors clearly assert that the city has been a fundamental cause of change in the family structure. Not only do urban families have lower birth rates, but the whole complex of urban structures and services have altered the nature of family life.

Okediji, Oladejo O., and Olu, Francis. "Marital Stability and Social Structure in an African City." NIGERIAN JOURNAL OF ECONOMIC AND SOCIAL STUDIES 8 (March 1966): 151-63.

This is a study of divorce among the Yoruba, in Ibadan, western Nigeria. The authors used 112 divorce cases. They assumed that the increase in divorce is due to changes brought by urbanization and industrialization. They tested and proved a number of hypotheses about these urban divorces:

1. Women tend to initiate divorce more often than men.
2. Women tend to sue for divorce on civil grounds, while men tend to sue on criminal grounds.
3. Most divorced women will remarry, and the second husband, probably a trader, will be wealthier than her first husband.
4. Divorces proceed more often against traders than against any other occupational group.
5. Divorced persons usually marry into polygamous homes.
6. Moslems have a higher divorce rate than other groups.
7. Divorced persons marry divorced persons.
8. In spite of the law, children in divorce cases go with their mother.

The authors believe that all these proven hypotheses confirm their assumption that urban-industrial society is making inroads into traditional patriarchal/patrilineal society.

Okonjo, Unokanma. THE IMPACT OF URBANIZATION ON THE IBO FAMILY STRUCTURE. Gottingen: Gottingen Philosophische Dissertation, 1970. 307 p.

This monograph asks how urbanization has affected the Ibo family structure. The Ibos are Nigeria's most recently urbanized tribe. The data used here is based on field work observation, conducted during 1965-66. The author compares three selected communities in eastern Iboland: one urban, one suburban, and one rural. He studies the economic organization of the households and advances the thesis that in a society where the basic unit of economic, social, and political organization is the extended patrilocal family, any trend which fosters out-migration carries with it change. This is true of permanent or temporary out-migration. Any change in the roles of family members causes a change in the family structure. It is upon the husband-wife relationship that urbanization has its greatest impact. The introduction of cassava into Ibo life and its acceptance by women allows women in a rural setting a greater degree of economic independence. While the mechanization of palm oil processing relieves women of much of their hard work, it also removes from women an extra source of income, since her husband retains the money from selling the palm fruits to the mills. In the city the Ibo wife can use trading not just as a source of extra income but also as a substitute for agricultural pursuits. Those urban women who do not trade find themselves more dependent on their husbands. This dependence is akin to a return to the precassava days. The move to the city entails a rise in the husband's status and a decline in that of the wife's. The husband is then able to command greater authority in the city. However, in general the physical isolation of migrant households from their tribal setting works to the woman's advantage. The urban husband tends to consult more frequently with his wife than he would have in the rural area and a greater closeness between husband and wife develops. Men in the city always refer to their village when they say "my family" while urban migrant women are referring to their conjugal unit. Urbanization, the authors conclude, has altered but not broken the Ibo family.

Oommen, Susie. PACE OF MODERN CHANGE: REPORT ON A STUDY BASED ON THE HOUSING COLONY OF THE INDIAN TELEPHONE INDUSTRIES, DOORAVANINAGAR BANGALORE, INDIA. Bangalore, India: Industrial Team Service, 1968. 56 p.

The author asserts that the Parsonian model of urban families does not fit here. There is a continuation of sex segregation in the home, but because of the need for income from female employment, men often have to work side by side with women. This was a study of working-class families.

Otero, Luis Lenero. "The Mexican Urbanization Process and Its Implications." DEMOGRAPHY 5, no. 2 (1968): 866-73.

Using a 1966-68 national sample survey, the author studied 2,500 couples and 300 social, political, and religious leaders. The author concluded that knowledge, approval, and use of birth control related to the type of rural-urban strata the individual came from. The common pattern in the large cities was that husband and wife made decisions jointly rather than by male imposition.

Palisi, Bartolomeo J. "Wife's Statuses and Husband-Wife Companionship in an Australian Metropolitan Area." JOURNAL OF MARRIAGE AND THE FAMILY 39 (February 1977): 185-91.

Family companionship functions have been greatly expanded with industrialization and urbanization. This study assumes that the level of companionship varies according to the wife's social status. The author predicts that a couple's joint participation increases with socioeconomic status and as urban residence increases, but that it decreases with age and with length of marriage. Suburban Australians were sampled and the hypothesis was supported. Recently married couples, high socioeconomic status couples, highly urbanized couples, and young couples demonstrated the most companionship.

Parkin, David J. "Types of Urban African Marriage in Kampala." AFRICA 36 (July 1966): 269-85.

The author attempts to lay out the different factors affecting the creation of different marriage types in Kampala, Uganda. In order to study urban marriage, the author notes, one needs to consider spouse's occupation, education, length of urban residence, and the number and types of previous unions. All of these must be related to conjugal role relationships. Of those women categorized as permanent wives, the largest number had been married in the rural area and then migrated with their husbands. Similarly, the largest number of temporary wives entered the union in the city.

Pauw, Berthold Adolf. THE SECOND GENERATION: A STUDY OF THE FAMILY AMONG URBANIZED BANTU IN EAST LONDON. Cape Town: Oxford University Press, 1963. 219 p.

The author describes a "triangle of forces" which underlie urban Bantu family life: Western, Xhosa, and urban forces. The author considers it difficult to decide which of these forces is dominant in setting marriage trends and family values. A mixture of church and civil marriages prevail; the lobola and premarital negotiations still take place. Relations between husband and wife are closer than in traditional Xhosa society, but the patriarchal form is still valued. Urban living has merely contributed to the process of westernization which had been felt back in the rural area. In the urban situation patrilineal ties have been lost, making way for more matrifocal arrangements. Desegregation of conjugal roles can be attributed mostly to urban influences.

Pool, Janet E. "A Cross-Comparative Study of Aspects of Conjugal Behavior among Women Of Three African Countries." CANADIAN JOURNAL OF AFRICAN STUDIES 6, no. 2 (1972): 233-59.

This article was based on surveys of Upper Volta, Ghana, and Nigeria from 1965 to 1971. The author posed various stages in the relationship between urbanization and conjugal variables. In the early stage where there is selective migration to cities by widows, divorced women, and other whose position does not correspond with rural traditional life, there is a lower urban completed family size. The second phase of the migration is a family migration. Here urban completed family size is equal to rural. Finally, in the third or urban stage, when migration has ceased, urban completed family size is lower than rural, partly because of modern contraceptive information. In all three of the countries examined traditional marriage patterns are still widely followed, but the data points out that with urban exposure new patterns of conjugal behavior develop. Education of women is seen as an important factor. In fact, the author notes that the strongest opponents of polygamy are educated women. They are also the first to accept contraceptive information, and they marry at a later age. While this is a small group, they are seen as influential in setting the pace for other urban women. The author concludes by noting that the forces of urbanization and modernization do not immediately liberate urban women and that the progress of birth control must be made in the context of meaningful economic and social change.

Rainwater, Lee. BEHIND GHETTO WALLS: BLACK FAMILIES IN A FEDERAL SLUM. Chicago: Aldine-Atherton, 1970. 446 p.

This is a participant-observation study of Pruitt-Igoe, a federal housing project in St. Louis, with 10,000 residents. The methodology included open-ended interviewing and horizontal and vertical analysis, with two surveys. In this housing project the mother was the source of authority and resources. It was a matrifocal community with a high degree of marital role segregation. The author feels that the economic marginality of the black residents was the cause of these particular family arrangements. These patterns were the result of the interaction of racism and a highly technological, segmented urban social and economic structure.

Reyes-Hockings, Amelia. "Newspaper as Surrogate Marriage Broker in India." SOCIOLOGICAL BULLETIN 15 (March 1966): 25-36.

Using fifty-two years of a Madras newspaper, the HINDU, which is written in English, the research studied 512 marriage advertisements. These advertisements illustrate and explain recent trends in urban Indian marital patterns. Arranged marriages continue for some urban Indians, but for others it has shifted to more formal, mass-oriented, urban-based means like newspapers.

Rosen, Bernard C. "Social Change, Migration, and Family Interaction in Brazil." AMERICAN SOCIOLOGICAL REVIEW 38 (April 1973): 198-212.

The author is interested in the impact of the industrial city on rural migrant family structure. As a result of his study of 167 lower-class Brazilian urban families, he concluded that the longer the period of residence in the city, the more egalitarian the relationship between husband and wife.

Ross, Aileen D. THE HINDU FAMILY IN ITS URBAN SETTING. Toronto: University of Toronto Press, 1961. 325 p.

This study cuts across caste, class, and language lines. The author finds that with urbanization has come a later age of marriage and upon marriage, the conjugal unit establishes a separate home much sooner. There are four observed changes in the role of the mother in the urban environment. Gradually she becomes the pivotal figure around which family life revolves. She must learn to assume responsibilities alone, which previously she shared with a group of other women. She may have to seek employment outside the home, in which case she will have to master social skills for sex-mixed situations.

Rosser, Colin, and Harris, Christopher. THE FAMILY AND SOCIAL CHANGE: A STUDY OF FAMILY AND KINSHIP IN A SOUTH WALES TOWN. London: Routledge and Kegan Paul, 1965. 337 p.

This is a study of 2,000 families of Swansea. The authors are interested in discerning various urban family structures. They conclude that the key relationships of these extended families are wife's mother to wife, and husband to husband's mother. The greater the level of the woman's domesticity, the stronger the extended family coheres and the more effectively it functions. The authors find a profound alteration in the roles and position of women in working-class families.

Rutzen, S. Robert. "Urban Life and Breast Feeding: A Sociological Analysis." SOCIOLOGICAL SYMPOSIUM 8 (Spring 1972): 65-72.

Studying women in Buffalo, the author asserts that breast feeding decreases in urban areas. The more time a woman spent in a city, the less likely she is to breast feed. Factors possibly contributing to this include urbanism, female employment, hospital childbirth, and formal education. The author feels that a much more significant factor may be the disengagement of women from home-based traditional systems which occurs most frequently and most rapidly in urban areas.

Rycroft, W. Stanley, and Clemmer, Myrtle M. A STUDY OF URBANIZATION IN LATIN AMERICA. New York: Office for Research, Commission on Ecumenical Missions and Relations, United Presbyterian Church in the U.S.A., 1962. 150 p.

Urbanization in Latin America has generally brought with it an improvement in the status of women, partly because of their earning power in the city. The numerical predominance of women among urban migrants has caused many women to get involved in irregular sexual patterns, including prostitution. The popularity of consensual unions in Latin American cities stems from the desire of urban Latin American women to remain free of male domination.

Safa, Helen Icken. "The Female-Based Household in Public Housing: A Case Study in Puerto Rico." HUMAN ORGANIZATION 24 (Summer 1965): 135-39.

Female-based households have a favorable predisposition towards public housing. Female-headed families usually view a move to public housing as a permanent arrangement. Public housing has contributed to the growing proportion of these types of households by weakening economic roles for men. The author, however, does not see public housing alone as the cause of matrifocality. The data from Puerto Rico is compared with data from Syracuse, New York.

Salaff, Janet W. "The Status of Unmarried Hong Kong Women: The Social Factors Contributing to the Delayed Marriage." POPULATION STUDIES 30 (November 1976): 391-412.

> The Dixon model which assesses the factors responsible for a rise in the age of marriage has been applied to Hong Kong women, ages twenty to twenty-four in 1973. Twenty-eight of these women were interviewed in depth. Of these, four delayed marriage because of the unavailability of suitable mates; twenty-one felt that marriage would jeopardize opportunities; only one felt that an early marriage would be advantageous. The author concluded that the age structure contributes to a woman's participating in the labor force, and early marriage would hinder her chances to meet personal and family obligations. The author observed that delayed marriage enhances women's status and is a good policy to be pursued by developing nations.

Sen Gupta, Anima. "The Role of Women in Indian Public Life in Modern Times." Ph.D. Dissertation, American University, 1959.

> This is a sociological analysis of Indian society, which seeks to understand the role of women in public life. The author asks if there has been an increased level of female participation in the society as a result of urbanization. The author looks at women's education, political participation, and labor force involvement as they relate to trends in social change. Especially significant here are changes in the family structure with modernization. The traditional large joint family is becoming more and more uncommon in the urban setting, where it is being replaced by small joint families. With urbanization and growing concern for individual freedom, there has been a change in the tone of family life and in the position of the woman within the family. Women have fewer family obligations in these smaller families.

Sennett, Richard. FAMILIES AGAINST THE CITY: MIDDLE CLASS HOMES OF INDUSTRIAL CHICAGO, 1872-1890. Cambridge, Mass.: Harvard University Press, 1970. 258 p.

> This study of Union Park, a neighborhood in Chicago, asserts that urbanization has changed the nature of family life. Some attention is given to the particular role of women within these families. Women have increased authority within the families, as men are relegated to the position of breadwinner only. The study also considers the work patterns of unmarried women. In discussions of married women's work the author notes that among wives of industrial workers, women often hold higher status jobs than their husbands do.

Southall, Aidan W. "Introductory Summary." In his SOCIAL CHANGE IN MODERN AFRICA: STUDIES PRESENTED AT THE FIRST INTERNATIONAL

Women in Urban Families

AFRICAN SEMINAR, MAKERERE COLLEGE, KAMPALA, JANUARY, 1959, pp. 1-66. London: Oxford University Press, 1961.

A great amount of attention is given to the changing status of women within the family in urban Africa. The new population centers have the greatest imbalance between men and women. This means that there is a great demand for women, allowing women to boost their economic status through irregular sexual unions with a number of men. The patchy data which has come indicates that there is a lower urban fertility. The author offers two possible explanations for this: (1) urban activities of women work against high fertility, and (2) the cities may be attractive to rural women who find themselves barren, and therefore marginal in traditional society. Another reason for the small families enumerated in urban censuses in East Africa, is that urban children will frequently be sent to the village to be raised by senior female kin in a tribal setting. The author states that it is important to distinguish between different types of urban women: those brought to the city by their husbands and those who came to the city independently. These two types will have different marital and economic patterns. In West Africa women in all categories are found as marketers and petty traders. In other African urban areas this is well established. In controlled towns and mining towns there is less room for individual enterprise, so women will be divested of their traditional trading role with no new substitute. Often the only feasible substitutes are illicit brewing and prostitution. Only among the more affluent urban Africans does the home provide urban fulfillment for women. Polygamy has been undermined by the economic bases of urban life, but the norms and values accompanying it have remained. The undermining of polygamy results in other expressions of the same pattern such as successive monogamy and sexual relations with a number of women. The West African tradition of independent female marketing provides a basis for adjustment to urban life, but there are many urban problems for women. For example, among Yoruba women in Lagos, the urban compounds correspond to agnatic lineages. The compounds survive a number of generations, have a good deal of authority over family life, and control female members. Women are hesitant to challenge the prerogative of the compound since it is still in a position to provide for them if their husbands cannot. However, an independent urban woman with her own source of money can establish her own household and does not have to marry for protection. Women's trading provides an important link between the rural and urban environments. Generally, women stay in the city longer than men, yet they are the major links to the rural and traditional life. There are different patterns of urban divorce throughout Africa. In northern Rhodesia, for example, there is no difference between the rural and urban divorce rates, while among the Yoruba, the city divorce rate is strikingly higher.

Southall, Aidan W., and Gutkind, Peter Claus Wolfgang. TOWNSMEN IN THE MAKING: KAMPALA AND ITS SUBURBS. Kampala, Uganda: East African Institute of Social Research, 1956. 272 p.

> Female emancipation in the city is viewed as a significant economic force in the society, even though within the Kampala families it is not considered reputable for a female to be employed outside the house. This emancipation of women is not just an outgrowth of urbanization but the culmination of a long process going back to the Ghanda land ownership and the introduction of cash crops. The authors disagree with the contention that emancipation of women is a factor in the instability of urban marriages. Also, the authors do not attribute this emancipation to the imbalance of the sexes, but to the absence of a recognized and agreed upon social system within which marital and sexual matters can be regulated.

Steyn, Anna F., and Rips, Colin M. "The Changing Urban Bantu Family." JOURNAL OF MARRIAGE AND THE FAMILY 30 (August 1968): 499-517.

> The author begins with a portrait of the traditional Bantu family situation. This is compared with the contemporary patterns in urban areas. The author stresses the breakdown of the family and the striking sexual imbalance in the urban setting. The status of the husband has been reduced while the status of the wife has been elevated. Legally this occurs through the equalization of husband and wife. In cities the relationship between husband and wife is freer, more informal. Widows in the city no longer belong to their husband's family and the custom of the levirate has been discontinued. Finally, polygamy has disappeared in the urban setting.

Sweetser, Dorrian Apple. URBAN NORWEGIANS: KINSHIP NETWORKS AND SIBLING MOBILITY. Oslo: Institute of Applied Social Research, 1973. 123 p.

> The author finds differences between urban men and women in terms of mobility. The author also discovers differences in importance between mother's kin and father's. One constant feature of urban industrial society is the consistent tendency for women to be more active in kin ties than men. The families could therefore be called matrilateral. This is partly because of the economic position of the husband in the city. These conclusions were drawn from a multistage probability sample of 500 urban Norwegians over the age of nineteen.

Trudgill, Eric. "Prostitution and Paterfamilias." In THE VICTORIAN CITY: IMAGES AND REALITIES, vol. 2, edited by Harold James Dyos and Michael Wolff, pp. 693-705. London: Routledge and Kegan Paul, 1973.

Prostitution was an attractive alternative for many women in London who were faced with poverty, low pay, and long hours in the factory. The swelling ranks of London prostitutes were observed by many foreign travelers to London. One reason prostitution thrived was the need among Victorian men. Middle-class men were marrying at later ages, and prostitution seemed to be a natural complement to the idealistic view of feminine purity for middle-class women.

Vatuck, Sylvia. "The Aging Woman in India: Self-Perceptions and Changing Roles." In WOMEN IN CONTEMPORARY INDIA, edited by Alfred de Souze, pp. 142-63. Delhi: Manohar, 1975.

Based on an anthropological field project in one of Delhi's "urbanized villages" (former agricultural settlements which have been encroached upon by the city), this article suggests that there has been little dislocation of women's roles and little important change in their self-perception accompanying the process of urbanization. The particular urbanized village under consideration has been incorporated into the city over the past forty years. Almost all of the women studied engaged in agricultural pursuits until recently. The particular caste in question owns much of the land so the elderly women are not faced with a marginal economic status. They have generally profited from the process of urbanization and have been able to enter into a period of relative rest and comfort.

_____. "Trends in North Indian Urban Kinship: The 'Matrilateral Asymmetry Hypothesis.'" SOUTHWESTERN JOURNAL OF ANTHROPOLOGY 27 (Autumn 1971): 287-307.

This study of an urban neighborhood in India shows a number of developments of the trend towards a matrilateral asymmetry among individuals who are traditionally patrilocal and patrilineal. This change is behavioral rather than ideological. The involvement of married women with the urban environment represents a broadening of permitted roles for wife and wife's kin as opposed to those limited to the husband's kin. These conclusions were derived from two multicaste neighborhood surveys in Meerut, Uttar, Pradesh, with a population of over 300,000.

Vogel, Ezra. "Democratization of Family Relationships in Japanese Urban Society." ASIA SURVEY 1 (June 1961): 18-24.

This article examines family relations in Tokyo, 1958-60. Urban wives have launched very little of a rebellion against their husbands. Urban Japanese families still have clearly segregated roles for husband and wife. The husband still maintains a position which is clearly prestigious.

Young, Michael, and Willmott, Peter. FAMILY AND KINSHIP IN EAST LONDON. Glencoe, Ill.: Free Press, 1957. 232 p.

> The working-class family centers around "mum." Daughters settle close by when they get married, and maintain an extended family over several households. This system provides support for women. It is, however, broken up with the construction of new housing estates which effectually bring husband and wife closer together.

Yuan, D.Y. "Marital Characteristics in Relation to the Rural-Urban Continuum in Taiwan." DEMOGRAPHY 5, no. 1 (1968): 93-103.

> The author asserts that there are few studies which view the relationships among community size, marital status, and family composition in non-Western cities. This study of Taiwan tries to isolate and explain local characteristics which may clarify the problem of city size and marital characteristics. Three types of administrative units are examined on a rural-to-urban continuum. The author found an increase in the number of single people--both male and female--with the increase in community size.

Section III

URBAN FERTILITY

Included here are works dealing with rates of urban fertility, the impact of contraception on urban women, and abortion.

Badenhorst, L.T., and Unterhalter, B. "A Study of Fertility in an Urban African Community." POPULATION STUDIES 15 (July 1961): 70-86.

This study is set in a Bantu housing project in Alexandra Township, which contains about 80,000 people, near Johannesburg. This community had grown rapidly during and after World War II and the authors were interested in measuring levels of fertility by interviews and questionnaires administered to randomly selected Bantu households. There are a variety of urban Bantu marriage patterns. The monetization of the lobola in the city helped bring about the breakdown of the traditionally stable African marriage. Men and women live together without formal marriage if they cannot afford the lobola. This may lead to lowered fertility rates, since women in such unions may make more efforts to avoid pregnancy than women in stable relationships. Urbanization has brought about greater contacts with Western ways of life, which the researchers expected would change fertility patterns. But in general there is only a slight decline in fertility, despite increased time of urban residence. A drop in urban fertility can be expected but it will be very slow.

Banks, Joseph Ambrose. "The Contagion of Numbers." In THE VICTORIAN CITY: IMAGES AND REALITIES, vol. 1, edited by Harold James Dyos and Michael Wolff, pp. 105-22. London: Routledge and Kegan Paul, 1973.

Birth control is an urban phenomenon. Urban working-class women are more receptive to birth control than the rural middle class. This is partly due to a greater exposure to ideas and life-styles associated with the more affluent. There is a brief discussion of the interrelationship among industrialization, urbanization, surplus female populations, feminism, and family planning.

Bash, Wendell H. "Changing Birth Rates in Developing America: New York State, 1840-1875." MILBANK MEMORIAL FUND QUARTERLY 41 (April 1963): 161-82.

This analysis challenges the traditional demographic generalization and transition theory by showing that rural fertility rates fell as rapidly as urban fertility rates in New York State in the mid-nineteenth century.

Bindary, Aziz; Baxter, Colin B.; and Hollingsworth, T.H. "Urban-Rural Differences in the Relationship between Women's Employment and Fertility: A Preliminary Study." JOURNAL OF BIOSOCIAL SCIENCE 5 (April 1973): 159-62.

Using statistical data for Egypt, based on the 1960 Census, the authors maintain that the child-woman ratio rises with levels of female employment in agricultural rural areas, but declines with increased urban employment. While the authors believe that more data is necessary, they do reach certain general conclusions. In cities providing ample employment opportunities for women, the birth rate does go down. In rural areas employment for women has the opposite effect. At low levels of female economic activity, there is little difference between urban and rural fertility rates, and in fact urban rates may be slightly higher. But when female employment rises to about 18 percent of the female population, the striking urban-rural difference emerges. As policy, the urban birth rate would be lowered if more jobs were provided to women.

Blecker, J.G.C. "Population Growth and Differential Fertility in Zanzibar Protectorate." POPULATION STUDIES 15 (March 1962): 258-66.

Of the two islands of the Zanzibar Protectorate, Pemba and Zanzibar, Pemba has a higher birth rate. The differing birth rate for the two islands, especially if focusing on Zanzibar Town, is due to lower fertility rates on Zanzibar. The author compares Afro-Arab birth rates in Zanzibar Town with Afro-Arab rates on Pemba and in rural areas of Zanzibar Island, as well as Asian birth rates in Zanzibar Town. The lower birth rate in Zanzibar Town may be attributed to a high proportion of single, widowed, and divorced women in the towns, as well as to deliberate family limitation among certain sectors of the urban population.

Bopegamage, A. "Ecology of Fertility in an Indian City." INDIAN JOURNAL OF SOCIAL WORK 27 (April 1966): 59-64.

This article looks at fertility patterns and their relation to other urban socioeconomic factors in the city of Poona. The author asserts that there is a spatial pattern in the distribution of human fertility rates. Those rates increase with the increasing distance from the main business center of the city. What variation is found in Poona can be attributed to socioeconomic conditions in the various wards. A high percentage of literate, more affluent home owners have lower fertility rates than poorer, nonliterate segments of the population.

Boyd, Monica. "Occupational Mobility and Fertility in Metropolitan Latin America." DEMOGRAPHY 10 (February 1973): 1-18.

Using data gathered between 1963 and 1964 on five Latin American cities (Bogota, San Jose, Mexico City, Panama City, and Caracas), the research attempted to correlate occupational mobility and fertility. After studying 600-800 women per city, who had been married for ten or more years, the author concludes that career mobility was not a significant factor in reducing fertility in four of the five cities.

Burnight, Robert G.; Whetten, Nathan L.; and Waxman, Bruce D. "Rural-Urban Fertility in Mexico." AMERICAN SOCIOLOGICAL REVIEW 21 (February 1956): 3-8.

In 1950 fertility ratios in Mexican municipalities related negatively to city size and to level of urbanization. Mexican fertility rates were subject to some differential effects of urbanization just as Western, industrial societies. The dominance of urban life significantly reduced the fertility ratio and offered a variable in fertility. The basic data came from the 1950 Census of Population of Mexico.

Caldwell, John Charles. "Fertility Differentials as Evidence of Incipient Fertility Decline in a Developing Country: The Case of Ghana." POPULATION STUDIES 21 (July 1967): 5-21.

Rural-urban fertility differentials are presented and interpreted by estimates of influence of other factors, including mortality, nuptiality, education, and religion. Using the 1960 Ghana Census as well as several earlier censuses, the author examined the four largest urban centers in the country. He concluded that delayed female marriage, which is associated with extended female education, is a significant factor in rural-urban fertility differences. He also noted that among higher socioeconomic groups, lowered fertility is also associated with conscious prevention of pregnancy. This is positively associated with extended female education, urban birth, and participation in first and monogamous marriages.

_____. POPULATION GROWTH AND FAMILY CHANGE IN AFRICA: THE NEW URBAN ELITE IN GHANA. Canberra: Australian National University Press, 1968. 222 p.

This is a study of popular attitudes towards reproductive behavior.

The generalizations are based on a survey of wives between the ages of eighteen and forty-four, and their husbands. The survey, conducted in 1963, was backed up by interviews. Among these couples, upper socioeconomic families with male-headed households contain women who married at a significantly later age. Husbands and wives who talk to each other about family planning are in general concerned about the national birth rates which are quite high. Urban elite families are closer to Western families in style and attitude than they are to rural Ghanaian families. In these families there are few marked differences between husband and wife, and most of the women under consideration here believe that four children per family is enough. Among the urban elites, family planning methods are widely known and extensively practiced. Two-thirds of the respondents with extensive schooling or with urban birth claim knowledge of some contraceptive measure. Information about the use and purchase of birth control devices is passed from woman to woman. The author concludes that contraception is most likely to be considered and used by second-generation urbanites, than by recent migrants.

Chinnatamby, Siva. "Fertility Trends in Ceyonese Women." JOURNAL OF REPRODUCTION AND FERTILITY 3 (June 1962): 342-55.

After studying 5,223 women, the author concludes that in Ceylon there are striking urban-rural differences in fertility. There is an inverse relationship between fertility and urbanization.

Cochran, Lilian T., and O'Kane, James M. "Urbanization-Industrialization and the Theory of Demographic Transition." PACIFIC SOCIOLOGICAL REVIEW 20 (January 1977): 113-34.

The article begins with a review of the literature on the "transition theory" and notes some of the problems surrounding the theory. In order to correct these problems the authors present a four-phase framework to interrelate the process of demographic change with urbanization-industrialization. Phase One, preurban, preindustrial society characterized by high fertility rates; Phase Two, with increased agricultural productivity there is an increase in fertility, considered a precondition for urbanization; Phase Three, urbanization and industrialization which are simultaneous and related but still distinct phenomena; Phase Four, the stage is set for a fertility decline, although there is disagreement in the literature as to when the decline began in Western Europe. The authors then advance five hypotheses to explain the decline: (1) the declining economic usefulness of children in an urban-industrial society; (2) the urban life-style characterized by small nuclear family units which are best adapted for city life; (3) the eventual lowered mortality rate; (4) the whole nature of the urban migration with its youthfulness; and (5) the movement of the new urbanites into the middle class which is linked to lowered fertility due to female participation in the labor force, the large proportion of single women, and the later age at marriage. The authors feel that no one factor caused the decline but all the factors are necessary. The expanding rural population of Phase Two is considered the most crucial link.

Collver, Andrew O. "Women's Work Participation and Fertility in Metropolitan Areas." DEMOGRAPHY 5 (January 1968): 55-60.

Using data from 1950 and 1960, gathered in eight countries, the author concludes that women's work is negatively associated with various measures of fertility. This is consistent with his hypothesis that a high rate of labor force participation by urban women tends to depress the birth rate. Communities with high levels of women's employment usually are correlated with low proportions of married women and low levels of marital fertility. The author asserts that there is a causal connection between work participation and fertility, which the literature has hitherto not adequately explored.

Collver, Andrew [O.]; Speare, Alden, Jr.; and Liu, Paul K.C. "Local Variations of Fertility in Taiwan." POPULATION STUDIES 20 (March 1967): 329-42.

The authors begin by noting that there has been a great deal of interest in the recent demographic experience of Taiwan, which was one demonstrating a marked decline in fertility since 1956. Data from household registration, representing 292 local administrative areas in 1961, are thus analyzed in order to delineate variations in Taiwanese fertility patterns. The data gathered here reveals that there is a strong negative correlation between total fertility and a series of indicators which measure social development and social communication. Fertility seems to vary most by differences in the fertility of women over the age of thirty at marriage. Any decline in total fertility can be attributed to a reduction of marital fertility for women of this age group. The adoption of family limitation is not limited to urban areas, but originated there and spread rapidly from the cities to smaller towns, and finally to the rural areas.

De Abuquerque, Klaus; Mader, Paul D.; and Stinner, William F. "Modernization, Delayed Marriage and Fertility in Puerto Rico: 1950 to 1970." SOCIAL AND ECONOMIC STUDIES 25 (March 1976): 55-65.

This study finds that no necessary relationship exists between modernization, including urbanization, and delayed marriage. It also finds that delayed marriage has a much less effective intervening role between modernization and lowered fertility. When a significant relationship exists, such as that between female education and delayed marriage in Puerto Rico in 1970, the relationship deviates from expectations. The authors thus found no direct effect of urbanization on fertility in any of the time periods. The authors felt that this was due to the ruralization of the cities and the development of subsistence urbanization. They used U.S. censuses of Puerto Rico data for 1950, 1960, and 1970 on fourteen subnation units (municipios), with multivariate regression analysis as the primary technique.

Dubey, Dinesh. Chandra, and Bardhan, Amita. STATUS OF WOMEN AND FERTILITY IN INDIA. New Delhi: National Institute of Family Planning, 1972. 49 p.

In India there has been no significant difference between the rural and urban fertility rates. The authors present a summary of much of the recent research to back up this conclusion.

Duncan, Otis Dudley. "Farm Background and Differential Fertility." DEMOGRAPHY 2 (1965): 240-49.

The author replicates earlier differential fertility studies which showed that fertility differences between farm and nonfarm couples are limited to couples in which one or both spouses were raised on a farm. The author maintains that these earlier studies dealt with too small of a sample. Using national data from the March 1962 Current Population Survey, the author surveyed couples with completed fertility where the wives fell between the ages of forty-two and sixty-one. The conclusion reached is that couples with farm background but high educational level do not differ in fertility from nonfarm couples.

Duza, Mohammed Badrud, and Husain, Imtiazuddin. "Differential Fertility in Pakistan." In STUDIES IN THE DEMOGRAPHY OF PAKISTAN, edited by Warren C. Robinson, pp. 93-137. Karachi: Pakistan Institute of Development Economics, 1967.

Using data from the 1961 Census the authors noted that East Pakistan, which was more urbanized, did not have a significantly lower fertility than more rural West Pakistan. When fertility is measured by child-woman ratio, a negative association between urbanization and fertility exists. This led the authors to assert that there is no relationship between urbanization and marital fertility in Pakistan. The general conclusion notes that the absence of any urban-rural fertility differences indicates that the urbanization experience of Pakistan has been significantly different than that experience in the West. Urbanization in Pakistan has not been accompanied by a general "urbanism."

Farley, Reynolds. "Recent Changes in Negro Fertility." DEMOGRAPHY 3, no. 1 (1966): 188-203.

Negro fertility has risen with urbanization. This is particularly
striking since urban fertility theory holds that the reverse should
have occurred. Traditionally, urbanization has lessened childbearing because of a number of factors, including the facts that
urban health was worse than rural health, and urban residents
were more likely to know about birth control than rural residents.
However, Negroes left rural areas and came to cities at a time
when urban health standards were improving. Moreover, since
blacks have not been integrated into the urban social system and
have had few opportunities for mobility, they have demonstrated
a slowness in establishing stable monogamous families with inten-
tional and deliberate birth control. The research here involved
the construction of cohort fertility rates, involving estimated annual birth rates; the number of women attaining the age of fourteen each year and annual birth specifics for the age of women
also had to be established.

Feldman, Kerry D. "Demographic Indices of the Squatter Problem in Davao
City, Philippines." URBAN ANTHROPOLOGY 4 (Winter 1975): 365–86.

The phenomenon of urban squatting has diverse cross-cultural di-
mensions. This study looks at families who live in squatter suburbs
rather than in inner-city housing. The men here are wage-earners
rather than peddlers. Families do have potential to become self-
supporting. High fertility behavior is a constant for all squatters
and the birth rate in Davao City is predicted to rise as the marriage age is decreasing. The number of miscarriages and deceased
children per mother is also declining.

Gardner, Bruce. "Economic Aspects of the Fertility of Rural-Farm and Urban
Women." SOUTHERN ECONOMIC JOURNAL 38 (April 1972): 518–24.

This article is based on a regression model. Both rural-farm and
urban women appear to be responding to income, wages, and
schooling in their fertility behavior. The conclusion notes that
there are significant rural-urban differences in fertility, but the
variables for estimated fertility function the same way for both
rural and urban populations of women. The only exception is
when race is taken into consideration.

Goldberg, David. "The Fertility of Two-Generation Urbanites." POPULA-
TION STUDIES 12 (March 1959): 214–22.

Conclusions in this article were based on 1952–58 area probability
samples, looking at couples with the wives over forty years of age.
Six separate studies yielded data on 1,072 second-generation urbanites and 442 rural migrants. The study shows the relation of
status measures to fertility and asserts that it depends on rural
background. The purpose of the study is to reexamine differences
within urban fertility patterns, with the assumption that any study

of urban fertility is made considerably more complex by the presence of recent rural arrivals. The general conclusion is that differences in the length of urbanism affect fertility more than do differences in religion or status. There were few differences in fertility among "pure" urban types. What differences did exist were considered statistically insignificant. The author attributes the differences in family organization in terms of husband-wife role to length of urban residence. The study focused on Detroit, Michigan.

Goldstein, Sidney. "Interrelations between Migration and Fertility in Thailand." DEMOGRAPHY 10 (May 1973): 225-41.

Looking at special tabulations of the 1960 Census, the article assesses the role of migration in the process of urbanization, and the relationship between migration and fertility. There was an increase in the proportion of urban growth which was due to natural growth, while fertility generally was lower for those in urban places. The relationship between fertility and migration varies depending on the measure of migration used. Nonmigrants in their place of destination and lifetime migrants have basically similar fertility levels, while the fertility levels of five-year migrants are significantly lower.

Goldstein, Sidney, and Mayer, Kurt B. "Residence and Status Differences in Fertility." MILBANK MEMORIAL FUND QUARTERLY 43 (July 1965): 291-310.

This study is based on Rhode Island and seeks to analyze the influence of city and suburban residence on fertility. The authors found conflicting results. The 1950 Census indicates that fertility on the fringes of metropolitan areas is higher than in the central city. More recent surveys, however, point to few suburban-city differences in the number of children born and the number desired. According to the 1960 Census of Rhode Island, the higher suburban fertility is limited to high-status suburbs.

Good, Dorothy. "Some Aspects of Fertility Change in Hungary." POPULATION INDEX 30 (April 1964): 137-71.

Spanning the period 1869-1960 the author analyzes rural and urban fertility rates. With industrialization centered in Budapest, the difference between urban and rural fertility rates grew. This was due partly to the phenomenon that in the industrialized city, marriage was less universal than in the rural areas. By 1910 small urban families had become typical.

Goodarzi, Abalhassan Moazami. "The Relationship between Urbanism and Urban Dominance and Fertility in an Urban Region." Ph.D. Dissertation, University of Maryland, 1966.

Using Wilmington, Delaware, the researcher attempts to prove the relationship between urbanism, urban dominance, and fertility by investigating the fertility performance of the populations residing in the various areas of an urban region. Within an urban region, the most highly urbanized residents and those who have the most contacts with the major urban centers have a significantly lower fertility rate than those residents who are farthest from the urbanized areas. The study develops a continuum of this relationship. On this continuum there is one central city--Wilmington, one protected hinterland, and one linear space dimension. The base of the hinterlands has the two largest urban places besides Wilmington. The author believes this to be a classic condition. Furthermore, the region has a uniform culture and economic base, as indicated by the colloquial names for the area: "Down State" and "Eastern Shore." The author then measures fertility by the ratio between the number of children under the age of five and the number of women aged fifteen to forty-four, as computed from the census data. The final conclusion is that fertility is inversely related to urbanism and urban dominance. Within an urban region this theme appears repeatedly. Fertility is higher in urban than in rural areas, higher in nonmetropolitan than in metropolitan areas, and higher in urban areas of less than 10,000 than in larger urban areas.

Gould, Ketayuan H. "Parsis and Urban Demography: Some Research Possibilities." JOURNAL OF MARRIAGE AND THE FAMILY 34 (May 1972): 345-52.

Many studies stress the lack of differences between India's rural and urban fertility statistics. The author charges that in part this may be due to the lack of a proper conceptualization of the "urban" variable. Similarly, the author feels that the studies have over-relied on census materials. The author chose to test this out with the Parsis and indigenous, since 1850, urban groups, whose members are integrated into an urban culture. Parsis women demonstrate a significantly lower fertility than other "urban" women in India. The fertility of Parsis women compares favorably with the low fertility of urban women in developed countries. The author then sets out to discover which conditions of urban life result in lowered urban fertility, for India. Among these are (1) an upward shift in the age of marriage; (2) the larger incidence of never-married women in their reproductive years; (3) greater knowledge of contraceptive techniques; (4) husband-wife accommodation in decision making; and (5) a lowering of the rate of infant mortality.

Halberstein, R.A. "Fertility in Two Urban Mexican-American Populations." URBAN ANTHROPOLOGY 5 (Fall 1976): 335-50.

Most of the literature on Mexican Americans stresses the high fertility level of Mexican Americans with large completed families. This generalization is explored against two case studies of Mexican-American populations in the Kansas City metropolitan area. Here the completed fertility in both, as measured by number of live births of women over the age of forty, is lower than the Mexican-American national average. The author believes that this is due to certain characteristics of the population structure and the demographic dynamics. The two urbanized populations are not geographically contiguous to other Mexican Americans. They are thus found in heterogeneous communities rather than in homogeneous enclaves.

Hareven, Tamara K., and Vinovskis, Maris A. "Marital Fertility, Ethnicity, and Occupation in Urban Families: An Analysis of South Boston and the South End in 1880." JOURNAL OF SOCIAL HISTORY 8 (Spring 1975): 69-93.

While ethnicity was a major variable in determining fertility, location in the city was the most important determinant. This was true even when ethnicity and occupation were controlled. Therefore the authors conclude that when dealing with fertility, urban areas should not be treated as homogeneous units.

Hashmi, Sultan H. "Factors in Urban Fertility Differences in the United States." In CONTRIBUTIONS TO URBAN SOCIOLOGY, edited by Ernest W. Burgess and Donald J. Bogue, pp. 42-58. Chicago: University of Chicago Press, 1964.

There are obvious differences in fertility within urban populations. Urbanism does not automatically lower fertility rates. Urban fertility has a strong positive correlation with level of income. At the same time, urban fertility also has a strong negative correlation with education and with female labor force participation. Race is an important factor and there is a significant white-non-white differential.

Hatt, Paul K. BACKGROUNDS OF HUMAN FERTILITY IN PUERTO RICO: A SOCIOLOGICAL SURVEY. Princeton, N.J.: Princeton University Press, 1952. 512 p.

This is a highly quantitative study which asserts that on no index of type of marriage was there a strong association with rural-urban differences and fertility. This takes into consideration age at marriage and legal versus consensual unions. Therefore urban-rural fertility differences must be explained by factors other than urbanism. The author also notes that the values of lowered fertility have touched rural and small town people simultaneously with urban populations.

Hauser, Philip Morris. "Demographic Aspects of Urbanization in Latin America." In his URBANIZATION IN LATIN AMERICA, pp. 91-117. New York: Population Branch, Bureau of Social Affairs, United Nations, 1961.

When considering all Latin American cities, there is a low urban fertility. It is lower than the fertility rate for the country as a whole. This is due primarily to the predominantly female nature of the rural-urban migration. The lower urban fertility rates seem to be unrelated to the degree of urbanization within the particular countries.

Hendershot, Gerry E. "Cityward Migration and Urban Fertility in the Philippines." PHILIPPINE SOCIOLOGICAL REVIEW 19 (October-November 1971): 183-91.

The Philippines does not demonstrate the usual pattern that rural migrants have a higher fertility than native urbanites. The author compares fertility levels of rural migrants originally coming from North West Luzon and Panay Island natives of Manila. The data here was garnered from three household interview sample surveys in 1966 and 1967. Immigrants to Manila did have a relatively low fertility rate which the author relates to the selective process of migration. That is, those individuals with higher aspirations for mobility tend to cluster among the urban-bound migrants and are therefore exposed to various influences which reduce fertility. This influence is nearly as strong as it is on urban natives. The author explains the deviation of the Philippines from the standard model for developed countries in terms of theories of different stages in the urbanization process. However, the general conclusion reached does not account for the methods used by the migrants to achieve this lowered fertility, even though the postponement of marriage and family planning cannot be used.

Hinday, Virginia Aldise. "Parity and Well-Being among Low-Income Urban Families." JOURNAL OF MARRIAGE AND THE FAMILY 37 (November 1975): 789-97.

The number of children (parity) has a strong negative relationship to the well-being of a poor family. Poverty is caused by factors other than parity, but the author maintains that policy should be directed at limiting the number of births to avoid further depressing socioeconomic well-being. Income level, public assistance, and number of months of maternal employment are correlated with parity. These relationships are not a function of changed welfare status, changed marital status, or recency of last birth. Additional children reduce a mother's ability to organize and run a household and limits a family's ability to save, although it shows no obvious effect on the ability to purchase durable goods.

Hutchinson, Bertram. "Fertility, Social Mobility, and Urban Migration in Brazil." POPULATION STUDIES 14 (March 1961): 182-89.

This article uses a sample survey of eight cities in south central Brazil, conducted in 1959 and 1960. The author found a close relationship between social status and social mobility. The lower the class of origin, the higher the fertility. The author concludes that if urban migration brings with it a rise in socioeconomic status, it will consequently bring with it a fall in fertility.

_____. "Induced Abortion in Brazilian Married Women." AMERICA LATINA 7 (October-December 1964): 21-33.

In 1963 the author conducted a sample survey of 2,498 married women in Rio de Janeiro. There was a high incidence of provoked abortion among married Brazilian women. It was high by Western European and North American standards. One in ten married women between the ages twenty and fifty had at least one abortion. This was equivalent to 9.2 percent of the population. The research has indicated that there is a temporary increase of provoked abortions with urbanization.

Iutaka, S.; Bock, E.W.; and Varnes, W.G. "Factors Affecting Fertility of Natives and Migrants in Urban Brazil." POPULATION STUDIES 25 (March 1971): 55-62.

For eight Brazilian cities, men and women over the age of eighteen were selected for samples. Migrants bring their fertility patterns with them to the city and in the city they tend to absorb the fertility behavior of the less fertile urbanites. There are more factors predicting migrant fertility patterns than urban fertility patterns, since migrants are a more heterogeneous group and are also experiencing many changes. Changes in migrant fertility patterns can be measured in one generation, and the second generation comes close to the "ideal" urban number of children.

Jaffe, Abram J. "Urbanization and Fertility." AMERICAN JOURNAL OF SOCIOLOGY 4 (July 1942): 48-60.

A number of non-European countries were studied to measure rural-urban fertility differences in the present. They were then compared with the United States and some European countries in the nineteenth century. While the author admits the inadequacy of the data, with only one exception rural fertility was always significantly higher. The author asserts that the availability of contraception in urban areas cannot be the answer, because Sweden demonstrated a lower urban fertility rate as early as 1760. One possible factor for rural-urban differences involves a "plane of living"--the sum total of all goods and services. Fertility decreases as a ratio of the standard of living to the "plane of living" increases. This article speculates that cities may attract more ambitious people or perhaps the conditions of social life in the city stimulate a desire for social advancement, which requires a lower fertility rate than rural areas.

Johnson, David Richard, and Booth, Alan. "Crowding and Human Reproduction." MILBANK MEMORIAL FUND QUARTERLY 54 (Summer 1976): 321–37.

Four hundred seventy urban Toronto women were examined as to the effect of neighborhood and household crowding on the probability of a pregnancy and on the probability that any given product of the pregnancy will not survive until the age of one. Crowding did not retard fertility nor did it influence fetal/infant survival. The authors contended that if crowding influences fertility it would be best studied elsewhere than in North America.

Kemp, Louise. "A Note on the Use of the Fertility Ratio in the Study of Rural–Urban Differences in Fertility." RURAL SOCIOLOGY 10 (September 1945): 312–13.

The author attempts to explain the wide variation between rural and urban fertility, focusing on American Negroes. The article notes that the variation between St. Helena, Louisiana, and New Orleans is great, and seems to be wider than for whites. Many New Orleans black families send their children to rural areas to live with grandparents in the country, so that urban statistics for number of children are in fact depressed while rural figures are somewhat inflated.

Keyfitz, Nathan. "Differential Fertility in Ontario: Application of Factorial Design to a Demographic Problem." POPULATION STUDIES 6 (November 1952): 123–34.

The research replicates for English-speaking Protestants the design developed for French Catholics in Quebec, which demonstrates that distance from cities affects fertility independently of the effects of income, education, and age. The object of the research was to determine whether the relationship between distance from urban areas and family size holds for English Protestants of Ontario as it did in earlier research for French Catholics of Quebec.

_____. "A Factorial Arrangement of Comparisons of Family Size." AMERICAN JOURNAL OF SOCIOLOGY 58 (March 1953): 470–80.

This is an example of the use of experimental design to study the effect on fertility of the interrelationships among age at marriage, ethnicity, income level, educational level, and distance from urban areas. The research found that distance from a city did indeed have a significant impact on fertility behavior. The impact

of the city on fertility, then, extended beyond the immediate
boundaries of the Standard Metropolitan Statistical Area.

Kiser, Clyde Vernon. GROUP DIFFERENCES IN URBAN FERTILITY: A STUDY
DERIVED FROM THE NATIONAL HEALTH SURVEY. Baltimore: Williams and
Wilkins, 1942. 284 p.

The general theme of this study is that urban fertility is low. It
is useful to look at the various subdivisions of the urban population. According to the findings here the most radical recent
change is by nativity. Far western married women demonstrate a
fertility pattern which is now only slightly higher than that for
northwestern married women of comparable age and length of urban residence. Urban married Negro women have a low fertility.
This contention is described as accurate even when the less than
adequate birth enumeration procedure is considered. When dealing
with urban Negro women, there is a problem of limiting the data
to married women, because there is a high rate of illegitimacy.
The author feels that class differences are not very important in
accounting for fertility behavior. Size of the community is offered by the author as an equalizing factor when considering the
fertility rates in the cities of the Pacific Coast. Group differences, it is held, in fertility diminish with the increase in city
size. The author notes that the spread of contraceptive techniques
and devices begins with the urban white, privileged families.

Knodel, John, and Pitaktepsombati, Pichit. "Thailand Fertility and Family
Planning among Rural and Urban Women." STUDIES IN FAMILY PLANNING
4 (September 1973): 229-55.

Based on a 1969 rural survey and a 1970 urban survey the authors
assert that the greatest need for family planning services is in the
rural areas, where family size is largest and contraceptive information is less readily available than in the urban areas. Fertility
for most age groups of women is higher in rural areas even though
urban fertility in Thailand is higher than urban fertility in other
cities, in developed areas. In terms of ideal family size, rural
respondents wished to have more children than urban respondents.
Rural-urban differences in age at marriage for women is also relevant. Urban women marry at a later age than rural women.
Urban women spend a greater number of years in school than rural women and this is considered an important factor. Urban marriage is a more expensive proposition since more urban than rural
newlyweds must set up a household independent of their parents.
Similarly, a larger percentage of rural widows remarry than urban
widows.

Kuznets, Simon. "Rural Urban Differences in Fertility: An International
Comparison." PROCEEDINGS OF THE AMERICAN PHILOSOPHICAL SOCIETY

118 (February 28, 1974): 1-29.

The article begins with a summary of fertility data from the late 1950s and early 1960s, focusing on lesser developed countries and applying to this data a cross-sectional analysis. A number of generalizations are drawn from this material. If the ratio of children under five years of age to the total population is high, or if the standardized birth rates of women of childbearing ages is high, there will be an excessive difference between rural and urban fertility. If the study is limited to the LDC's of Africa and South Asia, there will be a moderate rural-urban difference. It is most striking in the standardized birth rates for women in Latin America. In some African countries, urban fertility actually exceeds rural fertility. Although a combination of lowered fertility in urban areas with increasing urbanization should have lowered the total birth rate, there is no evidence of such a decline in the 1950s. Particularly significant for Latin America is the very rapid rate of urbanization and the marked urban-rural difference in fertility. Because of the narrow differences within some countries, intra-country data may be less revealing than inter-country data. South Asia and Africa form one pattern for fertility which may be attributed to the masculine nature of the urban migration, while Latin America and the developed nations represent another pattern. In the latter pattern, the predominantly female nature of the city-bound migration is relevant as an explanation.

Lee, Eun Sul. "Trends in Fertility Differentials in Kentucky." RURAL SOCIOLOGY 37 (September 1972): 389-400.

Studying the decades 1940, 1950, and 1960, the author notes that at the beginning there was a larger difference between urban and rural fertility rates than towards the end of the period under consideration. Urban fertility rates rose while rural rates declined, resulting in less difference between the two rates at the end of the 1960s. The data is viewed in terms of a child-woman ratio, with adjustments for undercounting and mortality of children, and using standardized ages of women.

Macisco, John J., Jr. "Fertility of White Migrant Women, U.S. 1960: A Stream Analysis." RURAL SOCIOLOGY 33 (December 1968): 474-79.

The author examined census data on fertility and migration for the period 1955-60. He studied data on women who moved between metropolitan areas, who moved away from metropolitan to nonmetropolitan areas, and women who moved from nonmetropolitan to metropolitan areas. For the total United States, migrant women had lower fertility than nonmigrant women. Of the three migrant streams analyzed, nonmetropolitan to metropolitan female migrants had the highest age-standardized fertility rate, while inter-metropolitan migrant women had the lowest. Through age twenty-four, nonmetropolitan to metropolitan migrants also had the lowest cumulative fertility.

Majumdar, Murari, et al. "Use of Oral Contraceptives in Urban, Rural, and Slum Areas." STUDIES IN FAMILY PLANNING 3 (September 1972): 227–48.

This study focuses on India's Howrah District, from 1968 to 1970. It seeks to measure cumulative continuous rates of use of oral contraceptives for women ages twenty-five to thirty-four, with four or five living children. In urban areas a majority of women who accepted the oral contraceptive attended the clinic prior to contact with the field worker, while rural women generally came to the clinic after one contact with the field worker. Slum women came only after the second or third contact. The highest cumulative continuous use rate for the oral contraceptives was among the rural women, while it was lowest among the slum women. Using the resources of the Family Welfare Planning Project, this study surveyed 1,429 urban women, almost all of whom were Hindu; 1,488 slum women who were 54 percent Muslim and 44 percent Hindu; and 1,304 rural women, two-thirds Hindu and one-third Muslim.

Marcum, John P., and Bean, Frank D. "Minority Group Status as a Factor in the Relationship between Mobility and Fertility: The Mexican American Case." SOCIAL FORCES 55 (September 1976): 135–48.

This paper presents contrasting hypotheses about the influence of racial and ethnic group membership on the relationship between mobility and fertility of urban Mexican Americans, based on 1969 data from Austin, Texas. One approach is a minority group status one. The other is labeled the underdevelopment approach. Both approaches offer explanations for fertility levels which are predicted to deviate from levels at which the group is. The former view implies great fertility changes with the greater integration of the group into the larger society. The latter view suggests greater changes the less integrated the minority group is into the larger society. These ideas were tested on Mexican-American couples, split according to generational distance from Mexico. The results show that there is more validity to the minority group approach than to the underdevelopment hypothesis as revealed by lower than average expected fertility on the part of couples removed from Mexico for at least three generations.

Martine, George. "Migrant Fertility Adjustment and Urban Growth in Latin America." INTERNATIONAL MIGRATION REVIEW 9 (Summer 1975): 179–91.

There are two areas of inquiry here: fertility differentials between native and migrant groups to see how migrants adjusted to city life, and direct as well as indirect contributions made by migrants to city growth. Three cities are viewed: Buenos Aires, San Jose, and Bogota.

Miró, Carmen A., and Mertens, Walter. "Influences Affecting Fertility in Urban and Rural Latin America." MILBANK MEMORIAL FUND QUARTERLY 46 (July 1968): 89-117.

The authors assert that intermediate variables are different for urban and rural women when attempting to understand fertility behavior. Among the important factors noted here are age at marriage, education, and family planning practices. Factors which seem to be less important in explaining urban-rural differences are age distribution and employment of women. Occupation of husband may be relevant but it has not yet been measured fully enough to be considered. The authors note that urban fertility has to be studied in conjunction with rural fertility patterns. Data for this is available through the Latin American Demographic Center (CELADE), which includes a series of two studies—a comparative study of urban fertility in seven Latin American countries, and the first phase of a rural fertility study in three countries. Among the preliminary generalizations advanced here are (1) differences do occur in urban fertility which may be correlated with general socioeconomic patterns of the respective country; (2) there are different rural patterns but the range is not as wide as for cities, and most importantly, (3) differences between urban and rural small town fertility are significantly relative to the average number of live births.

Mitchell, Robert Edward. "Changes in Fertility Rates and Family Size in Response to Changes in Age at Marriage: The Trend away from Arranged Marriages and Increased Urbanization." POPULATION STUDIES 25 (November 1971): 481-90.

The author sees two reasons for the way in which urbanization affects fertility and family size. First, urbanization is associated with a decline in the proportion of individuals marrying at young ages. Therefore there is a decline in the number of reproductive years. Second, the author considered the changing dominance and superiority of the male role, especially in the context of the declining number of arranged marriages. This, too, is seen as an urban phenomenon. Much of the data here was based on Hong Kong, with the universe for study being all married people living with a spouse in 1967.

Myers, George C., and Morris, Earl W. "Migration and Fertility in Puerto Rico." POPULATION STUDIES 20 (July 1966): 85-96.

An investigation based on special tabulations of the 25 percent sample of the 1960 Puerto Rico Census, this article asserts that

migration tends to be associated with fertility for various types of
marital patterns. Among them is the consensual union. This is
the case for urban, rural, and metropolitan residences. These
conclusions are not attributed to age composition among the various categories. But the authors did find that rural-urban and con-
sensually-legally mated differentials in fertility cannot be attributed to variations in migration patterns. Thus migrants had higher
fertility than nonmigrants; consensually mated women had higher
fertility than legally married women; and rural women had higher
rates of fertility than urban residents or metropolitan residents.
Except for women in consensual unions, fertility is lower for women
in the San Juan Standard Metropolitan Statistical Area than in
other urban areas.

Okun, Bernard. TRENDS IN BIRTH RATES IN THE UNITED STATES SINCE
1870. Baltimore: Johns Hopkins University Press, 1958. 203 p.

This monograph analyzes comparative historical fertility trends in
the urban and rural sectors and indicates the existence of parallel
movements. Refined birth rates vary inversely with the size of
the community. States with largely urban populations tend to
have small refined birth ratios. From this contention follows the
hypothesis that a rise in the proportion of people living in urban
areas can account for a decline in the refined birth rate.

Olusanya, P.O. "Rural-Urban Fertility Differentials in Western Nigeria."
POPULATION STUDIES 23 (November 1969): 363-78.

Rural and urban families in western Nigeria seem to have equally
stable relations. Rural families, however, have higher incidence
of polygamy. Urban women do not marry at a substantially later
age than rural women, but rural women do demonstrate more positive attitudes towards having a large family. In actual fertility
there seem to be few differences between urban and rural women.
This study was based on data collected in 1966 from two towns,
Ife and Oyo, and from five country villages.

Otero, Luis Lenero. "The Mexican Urbanization Process and Its Implications."
DEMOGRAPHY 5, no. 2 (1968): 866-73.

Using a 1966-68 national sample of 2,500 couples as well as
three hundred leaders of the social, political, and religious spheres,
the author concluded that knowledge of and use of birth control
related to the type of rural-urban strata in which the people found
themselves. In larger cities joint decision making was more common than imposition of male prerogative. Married couples in the
cities were more likely to know of, approve of, and use birth
control information.

Paulus, Caleb T. THE IMPACT OF URBANIZATION ON FERTILITY IN INDIA. Prasaranga: University of Mysore Press, 1966. 106 p.

The data in this monograph covers the period 1931-51. The author poses a number of possibilities: urbanization as the independent variable or fertility as the independent variable. Among the intervening variables he suggests literacy, migration, nonagricultural occupations, and standard of living. The data leads the author to conclude that urbanization is positively associated with increase in nonagricultural occupations, literacy, and migration. Yet no change in fertility patterns is noted with urbanization. Urbanization is accompanied by lowered child mortality, which produces a somewhat higher child-woman ratio.

Pool, Janet E. "A Cross-Comparative Study of Aspects of Conjugal Behavior among Women of Three African Countries." CANADIAN JOURNAL OF AFRICAN STUDIES 6, no. 2 (1972): 233-59.

In Upper Volta, Ghana, and Niger, urban educated women are the first to adopt contraception. They also tend to marry later. These women, although making up a small proportion of the total female population, are important since they set the pace for other women. The forces of modernization and urbanization do not immediately liberate women, and effective programs of birth control are critical in these three African countries.

Raina, Bishen Lal. "Fertility Status of Indian Women." In FAMILY PLANNING AND THE STATUS OF WOMEN IN INDIA: REPORT OF A SEMINAR HELD ON AUGUST 10-14 IN NEW DELHI, pp. 83-101. New Delhi: Central Institute of Research and Training in Public Cooperation, 1969.

Until the end of the 1950s there was only a small urban-rural fertility difference. When education began to be more widespread in the cities, the fertility level did begin to drop.

Rindfuss, Ronald R. "Fertility and Migration: The Case of Puerto Rico." INTERNATIONAL MIGRATION REVIEW 10 (Summer 1976): 191-203.

The effect of urban migration on fertility is particularly interesting when the areas of origin and destination differ dramatically in reproductive norms, with the former typically having a level higher than the latter. It is expected that urban migration would produce a lowered fertility than among nonmigrating contemporaries in the place of origin. It is supposed that migration itself and exposure to lower fertility norms will cause a lowering of fertility among the urban migrants. The author compares the census records of Puerto Ricans in the United States with Puerto Ricans in Puerto Rico. The supposition is not borne out, and the author found that there was essentially no difference between current fertility of urban island residents and of recent immigrants

to the mainland. Nor do these groups differ significantly from
long-time U.S. residents. What might have been originally attributed to the migratory process is actually a function of urban
residence.

Ritchey, P. Neal. "Effects of Marital Status on the Fertility of Rural-Urban
and Urban-Rural Migrants." RURAL SOCIOLOGY 38 (Spring 1973): 26-35.

Based on a 1967 survey of Economic Opportunity data, the research
generalized that white married women, aged twenty to forty-four,
who were rural-to-urban migrants, had only slightly higher fertility than indigenous white urban women.

Robinson, Warren C. "Urbanization and Fertility: The Non-Western Experience." MILBANK MEMORIAL FUND QUARTERLY 41 (July 1963): 291-
308.

The comparative analysis concludes that higher rural versus urban
fertility is not universal, and that the differential has lessened
with decreasing differentials in infant mortality. Where differential fertility is found, an important cause is differential nuptiality.

Rosen, Bernard C., and Simmons, Alan B. "Industrialization, Family and
Fertility: A Structural-Psychological Analysis of the Brazilian Case." DE-
MOGRAPHY 8 (February 1971): 49-69.

This study involved 726 mated women with proven fertility in
five Brazilian communities. After extensive interviews the five
communities were set on a rural-to-urban continuum. The continuum ran from one village to two nonindustrial cities to two industrial cities. Family size in the industrial cities was small on
all social strata, while in the nonindustrial cities, families in
the lower strata were larger than families in the upper strata.
Therefore the author concludes industrialization has an important
relationship to fertility and the effects of urbanization are felt
most strongly when associated with industrialization. Urban families were seen to be more egalitarian and in these families there
is greater consciousness of the need for and possibility of fertility
control.

Rosenwaike, Ira. "Two Generations of Italians in America: Their Fertility
Experience." INTERNATIONAL MIGRATION REVIEW 7 (Fall 1973): 271-
80.

The author compares immigrant Italian women with women in the
second generation. The comparison is limited to urban areas.
The author notes that it is critical to study the impact of the urban environment on Italian-American fertility, since the vast majority are concentrated in cities. He concludes that the high urban

concentration is a very significant factor and that the fertility of the cohort of Italian–American women is lower than the average of all women in urbanized areas. The author notes that ethnicity and religion also had to be considered.

Ryder, Norman B. "The Character of Modern Fertility." In ANNALS OF THE AMERICAN ACADEMY OF POLITICAL AND SOCIAL SCIENCES 369 (January 1967): 26–36.

This article attempts to point out the varying paths to low fertility in urbanized societies, with emphasis on the normative changes in parent–child relations. All urbanized and industrialized societies demonstrate a lowering of fertility.

Safilios–Rothschild, Constantina. "Sociopsychological Factors Affecting Fertility in Urban Greece: A Preliminary Report." JOURNAL OF MARRIAGE AND THE FAMILY 31 (August 1969): 595–606.

This study of Athens focused on two groups of women: 540 non-working women and 346 working women. For the urban family, the wife's generation in the city and level of education both demonstrate the degree of adherence to tradition or modern values. These were the most important factors used to predict family size.

Salaff, Janet W. "Institutionalized Motivation for Fertility Limitation." In WOMEN IN CHINA, edited by Marilyn B. Young, pp. 93–144. Ann Arbor: Center for Chinese Studies, University of Michigan, 1973.

Urban women have a higher rate of participation in communal affairs, therefore lessening their ties to the patriliny, especially when compared to rural women. Urban women are more likely to live neolocally and therefore have fewer obligations to their in–laws. Urban working women are forced to lessen the number of domestic responsibilities in order to be employed. Therefore all moves towards equal employment opportunities for urban women have an antinatalist overtone. All of these factors are important in understanding the motivation of urban women for limitation of family size.

Stanbury, W.T. SUCCESS AND FAILURE: INDIANS IN URBAN SOCIETY. Vancouver: University of British Columbia Press, 1975. 415 p.

This study of Indians in British Columbia makes no specific statements about women but does include general data on Indian urban fertility and marriage patterns. Fertility rates are lower for urban Indians than for Indians on the reservation.

Stycos, J. Mayone. "Needed Research on Latin American Fertility: Urbanization and Fertility." MILBANK MEMORIAL FUND QUARTERLY 43 (October

1965): 299-315.

> Much research on urban Latin American fertility needs to be done. Research on urbanization is complementary to research in macro-sociology, when it views the relationship of various types of cities, the degree of urbanization, and trends in urban fertility. Urban research is complementary to micro-sociology when it studies how urban life influences the patterns of belief regarding marriage patterns, household size, household composition, family size, contraception, and family planning. The author feels that research on the particular characteristics of urban-rural fertility differences is insufficient. He is particularly anxious to see studies of migrant and working-class women in order to conduct longitudinal studies.

Stycos, J. Mayone, and Weller, Robert H. "Female Working Roles and Fertility." DEMOGRAPHY 4, no. 1 (1967): 210-17.

> Using data from a survey conducted in Turkey in 1963, the authors note that rural women have more children than urban women. They seek here to study the relationship between women's employment and fertility, controlling for urban-rural residential patterns, education, exposure to conception within marriage. Generally no differences in fertility appear. Only in urban areas is there a noticeable fertility difference between employed and nonemployed women. A similar percentage of rural and urban women are employed, about 8 percent. Urban women generally marry later than rural women. One possible cause for the higher rural fertility is the ignorance of contraceptive methods.

Traver, James D., et al. "Urban Influences on the Fertility and Employment Patterns of Women Living in Homogeneous Areas." JOURNAL OF MARRIAGE AND THE FAMILY 32 (May 1970): 237-41.

> Based on 1960 U.S. Census data, this article compares and contrasts differences in fertility and employment of women in a sample of homogeneous counties. The conclusions reached are that both the size of the city and the distance within the metropolitan area from the metropolitan centers affect the proportionate number of employed females. The percentage of those employed consistently goes down with added distance and increases as the size of the city goes up. The fertility level increases consistently with the distance, but fluctuates irregularly with the increase in city size. The authors note that the vast differences which once existed between rural and urban patterns of female employment and fertility have lessened, even though they have not altogether been eliminated. The article is based on data from 81 counties surrounding three metropolitan centers: Atlanta (47 counties); Indianapolis (13 counties), and Omaha (21 counties).

Uhlmann, Julie M. Zinke. "The Impact of Urbanization on the Fertility Behavior of Papago Indian Women." Ph.D. Dissertation, University of Colorado,
1973.

The goal of this dissertation was to measure how certain social and
psychological influences work upon the fertility behavior of urban
Papago Indian women. The independent variables were migration,
preparation for urban residence, family size attitudes, and psychological modernity. The hypothesis dealt with the links between
these factors and fertility behavior as measured by dependent variables of children ever born, total number of pregnancies, use of
birth control, and fertility status. The researcher interviewed randomly selected women, aged sixteen to sixty-five, in the city of
Tucson, Arizona. The major technique of data analysis was multivariate analysis using multiple regression equations and partial
correlations.

Zarate, Alvan O. "Fertility in Urban Areas of Mexico: Implications for the
Theory of the Demographic Transition." DEMOGRAPHY 4, no. 1 (1967):
363-73.

The author tests two hypotheses based on Mexican census data and
vital registration information for the period 1940-60. The first
hypothesis is that urban fertility is inversely related to the portion
of the population of the city employed in the service sector of the
economy. The second hypothesis states that urban fertility changes
are inversely related to the proportion of the population of the
city employed in the service sector. The data provides little support for the first hypothesis, nor does it confirm the second. The
author states that overall fertility rises since 1940 in the cities
are found among certain sectors of the urban population. Changes
in economic condition seem to produce a rise in fertility rather
than a reduction.

_____. "Some Factors Associated with Urban-Rural Fertility Differentials in
Mexico." POPULATION STUDIES 21 (November 1967): 283-93.

The author asks what is the correlation of fertility to city size,
urban growth, sex ratio in reproductive ages, and nuptiality for
twenty-three urban and rural areas. City size was not related to
any of the variables. Those variables which are highly and significantly associated with urban-rural fertility differentials were a
lower percentage of growth in the urban areas between 1950 and
1960; a wider literacy differential; wider differential of age at
marriage; a wider percentage of the population being married;
wider sex ratio at the age of reproduction differential.

Zarate, Alvan [O.], and Zarate, Alicia de Unger. "On the Reconciliation
of Research Findings of Migrant-Nonmigrant Fertility Differentials in Urban
Areas." INTERNATIONAL MIGRATION REVIEW 9 (Summer 1975): 115-51.

After a selective review of the literature on urban fertility, focusing on the debates over differential migrant-nonmigrant fertility, the article examines the United States, Puerto Rico, and Latin America. The authors point out the various problems in research and the obstacles to accurate and full data collection. In order to make meaningful statements about migrant-native fertility differences in cities, it is significant to understand the social, historical, and cultural context as well as the different rates of fertility as they correlate with different stages of urban development.

Section IV

EMPLOYMENT OF URBAN WOMEN

Included here are citations on the type of work urban women do, the rates of labor force participation, the effects of urban employment on family life, female status, female self-perception, and fertility.

Boserup, Ester. "Employment of Women in Developing Countries." In PRO-CEEDINGS OF THE INTERNATIONAL POPULATION CONFERENCE, vol. 1, pp. 381-90. Liege, Belgium: International Union for the Scientific Study of Population, 1973.

> After rural-to-urban migration, women feel conflict concerning their roles as workers and their roles as mothers. The urban migration frequently brings with it certain developments that lead to a reduction of their participation in outside economic activities, while migration from countries at a higher stage of economic development is less likely to reduce female work input.

_____. WOMEN'S ROLE IN ECONOMIC DEVELOPMENT. London: George Allen and Unwin, 1970. 283 p.

> Women experience a radical change when they move from a rural to an urban area. This is due to the fact that in the rural area (focusing mostly on Africa, with some data on Asia, South and East, and Latin America) all economic activity is involved with subsistence. This cannot be transferred to the cities. In cities women have a narrower domestic range of economic activities than they had in the country. They have more time for nondomestic activities. In all of the areas under consideration, cultural and economic factors work together to determine the patterns of urban female employment. In Latin America, for example, the urban migration is heavily female because there is little need for large numbers of young women in the agricultural areas, because of the method of cultivation used. These women go primarily into service jobs in the city. The Arab nations demonstrate a pattern in which there is a very low level of female participation in development and in the economic life of either rural or urban areas. The opposite holds for Southeast Asia, where women are actively involved

in the process of economic development. In Africa women are extremely important in rural economies, but in the cities their employment activities are curtailed. The author presents a dynamic analysis of statistical comparisons among world regions and between sexes for many economic variables. One of the major arguments here is that the change from traditional to modern economic systems hinders rather than helps women's participation in the labor force. Modernization enlarges the gap in the levels of knowledge and training between men and women, and increases men's prestige at the expense of women's. The author proposes certain solutions, the most important of which is increased educational opportunities for women. Apart from the obvious effect this would have of reducing the gap between male and female productivities, it would also lead to the reduction of the birth rate. The author similarly believes that increasing female education and productivity would help accelerate the rate of development of the economy, which has been primarily based on male labor alone, since among other things, it might help keep the rural-urban migration within bounds.

Boyd, Monica. "Occupational Mobility and Fertility in Metropolitan Latin America." DEMOGRAPHY 10 (February 1973): 1-18.

In a study of married women in Bogota, San Jose, Mexico City, Panama City, and Caracas, the author determined that career mobility is not a significant factor in reducing the fertility rate in four of these five cities. For each city 600-800 women were studied.

Bulsara, Jal Feerose. PATTERNS OF SOCIAL LIFE IN METROPOLITAN AREAS: WITH PARTICULAR REFERENCE TO GREATER BOMBAY. New Delhi: Research Programmes Committee of the Planning Commission, Government of India, 1970. 456 p.

Among the noted characteristics which accompany urbanism in India, the author describes the entry of women into the urban labor force. These women come from a wide variety of classes. The descriptions of women in the work force of the cities are backed up with statistical data on female employment, as well as information on household work of the employed female. The author discusses the growth of female-headed households and their relationship to the movement of women into the work force.

Cohen, Abner. CUSTOM AND POLITICS IN URBAN AFRICA: A STUDY OF HAUSA MIGRANTS IN YORUBA TOWNS. London: Routledge and Kegan Paul, 1969. 252 p.

In spite of the usually described stability of Hausa urban family structure and supposed balance between men and women in the urban setting, there is a high incidence of prostitution here.

Many prostitutes are former housewives who have left or been left by their husbands and for whom there are limited economic options other than prostitution. A growing number of prostitutes are recruited from the ranks of the urban housewives. The pattern of female seclusion has led to the economic phenomenon of certain aspects of urban trading being left to women.

Collver, Andrew O. "Women's Work Participation and Fertility in Metropolitan Areas." DEMOGRAPHY 5 (January 1968): 55-60.

This is a study of eight countries, using census data from 1950 and 1960. The data here points out that women's work force participation is negatively associated with various measures of fertility. This is consistent with the hypothesis that a high rate of labor force involvement by women tends to depress the birth rate. Communities with high levels of women's employment tend to have an equally low proportion of married women and a low level of marital fertility. There is a causal connection between work participation and fertility. This has not been directly explored.

Collver, Andrew O., and Langlois, Eleanor. "The Female Labor Force in Metropolitan Areas: An International Comparison." ECONOMIC DEVELOPMENT AND CULTURAL CHANGE 10 (July 1962): 367-85.

The authors were interested in measuring the effects of female work force participation on rates on productivity as well as on levels of fertility. They studied urban female employment in thirty-eight countries: sixteen in Central and South America, seven in Africa and Asia, three in North America, two in Oceana, and ten in west and southern Europe. They noted that a moderately high rate of participation of women in the labor force is typical of the developed metropolitan area. The recruitment of women into the labor force will help create a decline in fertility levels by changing the nature of family life. It is necessary in most developing countries to effect this change since a high fertility rate is a definite obstacle to improving the standard of living, on a family-by-family basis. High levels of metropolitan female employment tend to be associated with a fairly unbalanced, high female sex ratio.

Economic Commission for Africa. "The Role of Women in African Development." In WORLD CONFERENCE OF THE INTERNATIONAL WOMEN'S YEAR: CONFERENCE BACKGROUND PAPER. Presented in Mexico City: 19 June - 2 July, 1975. Mimeograph.

The research notes that there has been a stepped-up rate of migration to cities by women in Africa. In Ethiopia, for example, urban women now outnumber men. Women in cities have a particularly hard time finding work, especially if they are poorly

educated, which is the case for many African women. In
West African cities where women for a long time were able to
find economic support through the monopoly of the market, certain new developments have undermined their only economic sus-
tenance: large-scale commercial operations have begun to displace
the women's market. Women traders have been unable to adapt
to this new development. Married women and single women in
cities have faced employment difficulties. The only avenues which
have been open are brewing (frequently illegally), baking, hawk-
ing, prostitution, and some other unskilled, low-pay, and low-
security jobs. Urban women, however, have somewhat better access to government-run child care programs than rural women.

Economic Commission for Latin America. "Participation of Women in Development in Latin America." In WORLD CONFERENCE OF THE INTERNA-
TIONAL WOMEN'S YEAR: CONFERENCE BACKGROUND PAPER. Presented
in Mexico City, 19 June - 2 July 1975. Mimeograph.

Generally, Latin American women have played only a marginal
role in the differential growth of urban middle and upper occupational strata. In much of urban Latin America educated middle
and upper strata women are able to combine occupation and family, because of the extensive availability of cheap domestic servants, women who are poor recent migrants to the cities. Women
of poor classes must be employed as well as shouldering full responsibility for their own domestic life. In addition, social services are provided for only a few. Among the most disadvantaged
in the Latin American cities, women are the chief breadwinners.
In Latin America there is a positive correlation between female
labor force participation and the evolution of an urbanized industrialized society. Eventually, this will bring with it a lowered
urban fertility rate and a higher degree of urban female education. However, at the present the larger, most urbanized, and
longest urbanized Latin American countries seem to have an even
lower level of female economic participation than the other countries. Among the former category are Argentina and Uruguay.

Foner, N. "Women, Work, and Migration: Jamaicans in London." URBAN
ANTHROPOLOGY 4 (Fall 1975): 229-49.

This article examines the changed status of female Jamaican migrants in London, focusing on two new aspects of their lives:
(1) the superior wage-earning opportunities in the city, and (2)
the separation from kin and close relatives. On balance, these
changes have improved the lives of these women, but their effects
are not entirely positive. The ability to earn a decent salary appears to strengthen women's claims to power and respect in relationship to their husbands and gives them the feeling that they
are more independent in England than in Jamaica. The absence
of kin tends to enhance women's power in the home, but adds to

the burden of child rearing. The concluding section delves into the implications of this study for the analysis of urban migrant women generally.

Fraenkel, Merran. TRIBE AND CLASS IN MONROVIA. London: Oxford University Press, 1964. 244 p.

This study of Monrovia, Liberia, contains an extensive description of the role of women as traders, including five case studies of such women. This income is crucial in the African capital because of the seasonal and sporadic nature of male employment. This situation leads to a new development among African women: greater female independence and authority.

Gadgil, Dhananjaya Ramchandra. WOMEN IN THE WORKING FORCE OF INDIA. New York: Asia Publishing House, 1965. 33 p.

The initiative in urban migration is taken by men rather than by women. In northern Indian cities women are a relatively unimportant factor in the labor force. The author infers, although he presents no specific data, that women who were actively involved in the agricultural economy cease to work when they come to the city. Using data from Bombay and Calcutta, the author describes the nature of women's employment patterns in the city, including a list of thirteen occupations where women workers are found. Among them manual workers are accounting for an increasing number. Importantly, over half of the employed women workers in Calcutta are widows. The divorce of the place of work from the home poses a great obstacle for the employment of women in cities in India. Therefore many urban Indian women are attracted to certain industries where work can be done within the home. This short book is a copy of a lecture delivered by the author at the University of Delhi.

Hass, Paula H. "Maternal Role Incompatibility and Fertility in Urban Latin America." JOURNAL OF SOCIAL ISSUES 28, no. 2 (1972): 111-27.

This study of maternal employment and fertility in seven Latin American cities notes that differences between cities are based on the peculiar characteristics of those cities. The author proposes that the crucial variable which will determine the relationship between maternal employment and rates of fertility is the extent of incompatibility between the role of mother and the role of worker. If this proposition is supported by the data, then employed women should have fewer children than nonemployed women. In Buenos Aires incompatibility is never related to fertility. Mother substitutes are readily available and there is widespread knowledge of contraception. Abortion is common and easily obtained. There is a widespread acceptance of nondomestic roles for women, either in the area of paid employment or elsewhere.

In Mexico City as in Buenos Aires, there is little association between role incompatibility and fertility, which is high in all sectors of the population. There is no widespread approval for nondomestic roles for women. Those women who work do so for purely economic reasons. This economic need is in part caused by excessively high fertility. In Rio de Janeiro, Bogota, and Caracas, labor force participation for women seems to attract precisely those women who do not want large families. In San Jose and Panama City there has been a decline in fertility. Wives are frequently employed outside the home. Employed women marry later than in other cities, attain a higher level of education, and have a greater level of urban experience than nonemployed women.

Hellmann, Ellen. ROOIYARD: A SOCIOLOGICAL SURVEY OF AN URBAN NATIVE SLUM YARD. Cape Town: Oxford University Press, 1948. 125 p.

The research on the Rooiyard area of Johannesburg was carried out in 1933. The author contends that the Rooiyard natives were not part of a stable urban population, but shifted in and out of the city. The increase in the urban native female population reflected the increase in urban employment opportunities for natives. With greater employment, the natives were set into the processes of assimilation into the urban environment and detribalization. This then became a more permanent form of urbanization. The author noted a high degree of family breakup. This is partly because urban women cannot adequately take care of their children in the city slum so they will send them back to the rural village. This is done both for economic utility and for moral upbringing. Urban women in Rooiyard are able to make money. The most important source of their income comes from brewing beer. There are also a significant number of domestic jobs, frequently referred to as "washing jobs." Urban conditions have reaffirmed the economic importance of women but have altered the nature of their work and their economic contribution. Beer brewing has led to the creation of women's mutual benefit organizations. Women traders have joined together into a "stock fair" which serves both economic and social functions. The author sees these as the only examples of a spirit of cooperation among urban women. Additional information about the changes in women's lives with urbanization is given. Most Rooiyard natives have dropped many traditional tribal customs with the conspicuous exception of those customs surrounding childbirth. This is especially true in terms of the practice of seclusion of the woman and her newborn baby. Similarly, the author observes that under urban conditions the lobola is becoming a purchase which is a major deviation from the purposes of the lobola in the tribal area. The study is generally descriptive and impressionistic. It was published under the auspices of the Rhodes–Livingstone Institute.

Hunt, Chester L. "Female Occupational Roles and the Urban Sex Ratios in the United States, Japan, and the Philippines." SOCIAL FORCES 43 (March 1965): 407-16.

The low sex ratio in U.S. urban areas has been attributed to industrialization and the demand for women workers in the cities. Japan has had no disproportionate sex ratio in spite of its industrial development. The Philippines, on the other hand, has had a sex ratio similar to that in the United States without having gone through advanced industrialization. This article examines education of women and employment of women in the urban areas of these three countries. The author proposes that factors other than industrialization are responsible for the movement of women into the cities and the types of occupations available for them there. The Japanese model is one in which women are subordinate in spite of industrialization, while the United States has demonstrated a commitment to sex equality, which in turn has produced a feminine work pattern along supplemental lines. In the Philippines the minor advances of industrialization have provided more opportunities for female employment because of a traditional concept of the feminine role which has generally been favorable to female employment outside the home. Most of this study concentrates on the Philippines and uses the United States and Japan for comparative purposes. The data comes from the 1960 Census of the Philippines.

Kapur, Promilla. MARRIAGE AND THE WORKING WOMAN IN INDIA. Delhi: Vikas Publications, 1970. 525 p.

Although there is little explicit discussion of urbanization, most of the research and data is based on urban women. This study involves an analysis of the factors in the levels of marital adjustment when the wife is employed outside the home. There is some specific data on urban, educated women and an implicit understanding that urbanization has been an important factor in motivating large numbers of Indian women to want to continue working beyond marriage. The author sees a complex set of reasons for this wish, only part of which is attributed to financial need.

Klein, Viola. BRITAIN'S MARRIED WOMEN WORKERS. London: Routledge and Kegan Paul, 1965. 166 p.

When measuring the number of married women workers the author found that rural areas had the lowest percentage of employed married women. Towns of 50,000 to 250,000 had the highest, employed full-time. In terms of part-time employment, however, there was very little difference, although small towns had somewhat fewer opportunities than large cities or rural areas.

Krapf-Askari, Eva. YORUBA TOWNS AND CITIES: AN ENQUIRY INTO

THE NATURE OF URBAN SOCIAL PHENOMENA. Oxford: Clarendon Press, 1969. 195 p.

> This study of a West African tribe in a number of cities and towns, including Ibadan, Ife, Oyo, and Ilorin, describes the economic activities of women. The author observed that town life allows greater economic specialization. As a result, a women's economic sector emerges, specializing in trading and in the crafts.

Legerman, Caroline J. "Haitian Peasant, Plantation, and Urban Lower Class Family and Kinship Organization: Observation and Comments." In PAPERS OF THE CONFERENCE ON RESEARCH AND RESOURCES OF HAITI, edited by Richard P. Schaedel, pp. 71-84. New York: Research Institute for the Study of Man, 1969.

> In the urban areas there are many professional or semiprofessional prostitutes. For urban women, employment opportunities mean a reduced economic dependence on men. In the Haitian urban areas, there are usually more jobs available to lower-class women than to lower-class men. This study also appeared as "Observation on Family and Kinship Organization in Haiti." In THE HAITIAN PO-TENTIAL: RESEARCH AND RESOURCES OF HAITI, edited by Vera Rubin and Richard P. Schaedel. New York: Columbia University, Teachers College Press, 1975.

McCall, Daniel F. "The Effect on Family Structure of Changing Economic Activities of Women in a Gold Coast Town." Ph.D. Dissertation, Columbia University, 1956.

> The author asserts that subordination and fidelity are related to changes in women's economic activities. In rural agricultural areas women are expected to be economically productive by farm-ing. For town women farming is unavailable so women turn to-wards marketing as the functional equivalent. While trading has certain positive economic functions, it is also dysfunctional to the old family structure. Trading puts women's economic activities beyond the direct supervision of the husband. In farming, men are able to chaperone their wives while working. But in trading, economic success depends on knowing about prices, seasonal prod-ucts, and the like. In the Gold Coast town, women possess this specialized trading knowledge. Men do not have access to this knowledge. Men therefore cannot interfere with their trading wives without threatening the family's economic situation. Women have total control of the market situation and this is important in putting women in town into a superordinate position. Women do not actively strive to change their status in the family relative to men. They merely want to replace farming with a more conven-ient economic activity--trading. This, however, results in changes in the family, since family structure and economic roles are con-nected.

_____. "Trade and the Role of Wife in a Modern West African Town." In SOCIAL CHANGE IN MODERN AFRICA, edited by Aidan W. Southall, pp. 286-99. London: Oxford University Press, 1961.

In traditional Akan society, most farm work is done by women. Women also have some limited activity in the area of trading. Husband and wife maintain separate accounts in addition to the general family pool. This, according to the author, signifies the tenuousness of the institution of marriage in traditional Akan society. In general, lineage ties are stronger than marital ties and the husband is in a superordinate position. Yet, in the towns of Ghana, Akan women are primarily traders and exert only a minimum of effort to return to the village and work their husbands' farm land. In the market women handle a wide variety of goods. Men in the city experience a decline of activity and participate less in trade than they did in the country. The author asserts that the size of the town is important in determining the level of women's marketing activity, as is the number of women traders in the town. Of the newcomers to the city among the women traders, the majority were wives in polygamous situations. Husbands do not usually control the products of their wives' labor in the city, as they did in agriculture. The general conclusion of this article, which was based on both survey data and descriptive material, is that urbanization and the economic role of the city woman in trading has diminished the male dominance both in economic and sexual activities.

McLaughlin, Virginia Yans. "Patterns of Work and Family Organization: Buffalo's Italians." JOURNAL OF INTERDISCIPLINARY HISTORY 2 (Autumn 1971): 299-314.

Urban employment opportunities had little effect on the traditional male-female roles among southern Italians in Buffalo. Women opted for those jobs which did not challenge well-established family patterns. They took in boarders and engaged in work that could be done within the home, like making buttonholes and artificial flowers. Frequently they would leave the city to work in the fruit orchards and canneries, but they took their children with them, keeping the family unit intact. If they had to work in a factory, they would tend to work in one owned by a relative or a compatriot from southern Italy.

MacLean, Annie Marion. WAGE EARNING WOMEN. New York: Macmillan, 1910. 202 p. Reprint. New York: Arno Press, 1968.

This geographically organized survey of employed women is heavily statistical. It compares the conditions of women's work in the urban setting with the conditions of rural women's employment.

Marris, Peter. AFRICAN CITY LIFE. Kampala, Uganda: Transition Books, 1967. 260 p.

One of the effects of urban migration on the economic position of women is a high degree of married women's work outside the home. Since urban African marriage lacks a stable base, due in part to the insecurity of a guaranteed livelihood for men, women are forced to seek some form of economic insurance for themselves and their children. Due to an increased economic role for urban women, women in the city have a more independent status, at the expense of the traditional protection.

Myers, George C. "Labor Force Participation of Suburban Mothers." JOURNAL OF MARRIAGE AND THE FAMILY 26 (August 1964): 306-11.

In this exploratory study, the author suggests that one of the variables in determining maternal employment is the type of suburb. Three types of suburban communities were studied: (1) upper middle-class residential suburbs with no major employment facilities; (2) more heterogeneous, but mostly lower middle-class suburbs also without major employers; and (3) an industrial suburb. In this case the research focused on an industrial suburb which housed an airplane plant. The author notes that while differences in employment opportunities in the three communities appear to be inadequate as the key variable in explaining the pattern, the nature of the suburban community does in fact play an important role. All three suburbs had a high level of maternal employment. The author concludes, "In terms of historical perspective, it may be that the isolated nuclear urban family was a unique phenomenon during early periods of urbanization and that today the modified extended family characterizes urban and perhaps suburban settings."

Ogburn, William F., and Nimkoff, Meyer Francis. TECHNOLOGY AND THE CHANGING FAMILY. Boston: Houghton Mifflin Co., 1955. 329 p.

Most jobs available for women are located in urban areas, since most jobs considered suitable have come through industry and government. Cities render important social services for employed women.

Ottenberg, Phoebe V. "The Changing Economic Position of Women among the Afikpo Ibo." In CONTINUITY AND CHANGE IN AFRICAN CULTURES, edited by William R. Bascom and Melville J. Herskovits, pp. 205-33. Chicago: University of Chicago Press, 1959.

Semiurban women in the "palm belt" are compared with women of the Ibo tribe in the urban setting. In the semiurban state agriculture is still important, but is not central. There is a high degree of population density. Women here have a fairly high income. That income is greater than that of women in the totally nonurbanized Ibo area, but it is a less stable income. Urban Ibo women divide occupationally along educational lines. The largest proportion of the urban women are market traders.

They may also be middlemen in the fish and yam trade, money-lenders and pawnbrokers, and dressmakers. Prostitution as an occupation has increased since the British ruled. The author contends that the type of residence is not the only factor in determining the direction of women's employment. Urban women may farm or process palms into salable products. Education for women, as well as for men, seems to be a more important factor than the type of residence. However, more educated women are located in the cities than in the rural areas. They are found in positions as teachers and accredited midwives.

Petrelli, Richard L. "The Regulation of French Midwifery During the Ancien Régime." JOURNAL OF THE HISTORY OF MEDICINE AND ALLIED SCIENCES 26 (July 1971): 276-92.

    The author notes that one cause of the regulation and eventual decline of midwifery was the rise of centralized municipal governments.

Powell, Dorian L. "Female Labor Force Participation and Fertility: An Exploratory Study of Jamaican Women." SOCIAL AND ECONOMIC STUDIES 25 (September 1976): 234-58.

    The author notes that Jamaica has a high level of working women and also a high level of fertility. The data suggests a strong positive relationship between urban residence and female work force participation. This is true for both eastern and western Jamaica. The author also studied various types of female unions with men, including marriage. Women in no unions have higher rates of work than those in unions. Disrupted unions generally lead to female labor force participation.

Provencher, Ronald. TWO MALAY WORLDS: INTERACTION IN URBAN AND RURAL SETTINGS. Berkeley: Center for South and Southeast Asia Studies, University of California, 1971. 211 p.

    This monograph compares Kuala Lumpur, a multiethnic city with a recently settled rubber estate, inhabited primarily by Sumatrans. Among the topics covered and compared were sex socialization and female employment. The author found a low level of urban female employment, especially among the wives of homeowners. Urban women usually had a lower level of responsibility than rural women.

Roy, Prodypto. "Maternal Employment and Adolescent Roles: Rural-Urban Differentials." MARRIAGE AND FAMILY LIVING 23 (November 1961): 340-49.

    The author contends that rural families seem to benefit more from maternal employment than do urban families. Women in all marital situations in urban areas are more likely to be employed than those in rural areas. In rural areas nonfarm resident women are more likely to be employed than farm residents. Children of urban employed mothers participate less than their counterparts with nonemployed mothers in out-of-school activities. The employment of town mothers lowers the academic performance and aspirations of their children and raises those of rural children of employed mothers. These generalizations were derived from data garnered from 1,086 questionnaires of high school students in two counties of northeast Washington State.

Salaff, Janet W. "Institutionalized Motivation for Fertility Limitation." In WOMEN IN CHINA, edited by Marilyn B. Young, pp. 93-144. Ann Arbor: Center for Chinese Studies, University of Michigan, 1973.

This article presents statistics on the proportion of women in the urban work force, on the percentage of women who are employed outside the home, and on the breakdown of women by type of position (managerial, white-collar, and so on). Urban working-class women are forced to lessen the number of domestic responsibilities in order to be employed. Employment for women in the city tends to have an antinatalist orientation.

Sidel, Ruth. FAMILIES OF FENG SHUNG: URBAN LIFE IN CHINA. London: Penguin Books, 1974. 166 p.

Based on the author's travels to China, this study depicts the integration of home, work, political life, and urban society. Many neighborhood services are provided for working women and there is an equalization of work and family roles for women, stemming directly from the ideology. There is some statistical material, but generally the book is descriptive.

Skinner, Elliott P. AFRICAN URBAN LIFE: THE TRANSFORMATION OF OUAGADOUGOU. Princeton, N.J.: Princeton University Press, 1974. 487 p.

In the process of urbanization many female practices, particularly those involving women's economic roles, which were acceptable in the rural village, are no longer acceptable in the city. A major example of this is brewing and selling beer. This change often leads to marital conflict, and eventually to divorce. In the city, women and wives are no longer economic and legal wards of their husbands and male kin.

Smith, Margo L. "Domestic Service as a Channel of Upward Mobility for the Lower-Class Woman: The Lima Case." In FEMALE AND MALE IN LATIN AMERICA: ESSAYS, edited by Ann Pescatello, pp. 191-207. Pittsburgh: University of Pittsburgh Press, 1973.

This study of rural-to-urban migrant women notes that domestic service plays a key role in the assimilation and adjustment of poor young country girls into the urban lower class. Through domestic service the young migrant servant girl is exposed to more of the urban environment than her nonservant counterparts. For example, it is within the context of urban domestic service that the servant girl learns how to communicate completely in Spanish.

Speare, Alden; Speare, Mary C.; and Lin, Hui-Shend. "Urbanization, Non-familial Work, Education and Fertility in Taiwan." POPULATION STUDIES 27 (July 1973): 323-34.

The authors raise the question of which of the complex variables associated with development and modernization are responsible for the reduction of fertility. The three variables which are raised most frequently in the literature are (1) increased education, (2) urbanization, and (3) paid employment for women. The authors then attempt to isolate the independent effects of these three variables in terms of attitudes towards fertility in Taiwan. Taiwan was chosen because it is one of the most rapidly developing of the less developed countries and is in the middle stage of the demographic transition in which death rates and birth rates plummet. Young women with varying exposures to urban life were researched. (Altogether the investigators surveyed 3,929 women between eighteen and twenty-nine on a cross-national sample.) Education emerged as the most important factor in determining fertility attitude and behavior. Education has an inverse relationship to desired number of children. Exposure to urban life has only a small independent effect on desired fertility once education is controlled. Because of exposure from mass media in the countryside, women in nonurban environments are made aware of family planning programs also.

Stycos, J. Mayone, and Weller, Robert H. "Female Working Roles and Fertility." DEMOGRAPHY 4, no. 1 (1967): 210-17.

Using survey data from Turkey from 1963 the authors assert that rural women have more children than urban women. The article attempts to study the relationship between female employment and fertility, by controlling for urban-rural residence, education, and exposure to contraception within marriage. Only in urban areas was there a noticeable fertility difference between employed and nonemployed women. A similar percentage of 8 percent of both rural and urban women were employed outside the home.

Touba, Jacqueline Rudolph. "The Relationship between Urbanization and the Changing Status of Women in Iran, 1956-1966." IRANIAN STUDIES 5, no. 1 (1972): 25-36.

Based on comparisons between the 1956 and 1966 censuses with special attention on employment and education of urban women in the cities of Tehran, Esfahan, Tabriz, Abadan, and Shiraz, this article notes that there are important and interesting differences among the cities. In the decade under consideration, the proportion of women in production and crafts decreased, while that of women in the professions and in technical jobs increased. However, the overall percentage of women in the labor force has hardly changed from between 8 and 9 percent.

Traver, James D., et al. "Urban Influences on the Fertility and Employment Patterns of Women Living in Homogeneous Areas." JOURNAL OF MARRIAGE AND THE FAMILY 32 (May 1970): 237-41.

This study of eighty-one U.S. counties which are surrounding three metropolitan centers compares and contrasts these homogeneous areas in terms of fertility and female employment. The conclusion reached is that both size of city and the distance from the metropolitan center affect the proportion of employed females. The percentage of those women who are employed consistently goes down with added distance, and increases as the size of the city goes up.

Trowbridge, James W. URBANIZATION IN JAMAICA. New York: International Urbanization Survey, Ford Foundation, n.d. 30 p.

The author notes that a large proportion of the rural migrants to Kingston are women. Of these women a very large number are employed as domestics once they settle in the city.

United Nations. Department of Economic and Social Affairs. REPORT OF THE INTERREGIONAL MEETING OF EXPERTS ON THE INTEGRATION OF WOMEN IN DEVELOPMENT, UNITED NATIONS HEADQUARTERS, 19-28 JUNE, 1972. New York: United Nations, 1973.

Urban unemployment is seen as one of the most significant obstacles to industrial employment of women. Urban employment recruitment policies favor men. Therefore the man's income must be able to support the entire family. This is complicated, however, by the high birth rate and the lack of adequate jobs for females. Despite higher urban wages for men, urban families are not able to save much and their capacity for paying taxes is minimal. Generally the report notes that if the cityward migration does not slow down and if women continue to be deprived of employment opportunities in the city, there will be proportionately fewer economically productive members of the society. Because of shrinking female earnings, men will be burdened by more dependents and women in the towns will be forced to compete bitterly among themselves for the few job opportunities. This report was based on data from Denmark, Indonesia, Sierra Leone, Yugoslavia, and Venezuela.

_____. STATUS OF WOMEN AND FAMILY PLANNING: REPORT OF THE
SPECIAL RAPPORTEUR APPOINTED BY THE ECONOMIC AND SOCIAL
COUNCILS UNDER RESOLUTION 1326. New York: United Nations, 1975.

Women's paid employment is more likely to be incompatible with
raising a family in an urban area than in a rural. Urban women
are more likely to learn about birth control and more likely to
have access to family planning centers. Studies of Guatemala,
India, Jordan, the Philippines, and the Syrian Arab Republic demonstrate that the negative relationship between female employment
and fertility is clearest in cities, among nonagricultural workers
and in conjunction with education. In rural areas, employment
rarely delays marriage or reduces fertility. One Egyptian study
found that women who had greater freedom of movement outside
the house and a greater authority within the family said they
would use contraception even if their husband disapproved. This
independence was linked to education, female employment, and
urban residence. In Africa and Asia, urban migrants were mostly
men while in Europe and the Americas women constituted the majority of cityward migrants.

Van Allen, Judith. "African Women, 'Modernization,' and National Libera-
tion." In WOMEN: A COMPARATIVE STUDY, edited by Lynne B. Iglitzen
and Ruth Ross, pp. 25–54. Oxford: Clio Books, 1976.

Most unmarried women in African cities are illiterate and subsequently have no access to white-collar occupations. Even when
they are educated, employment preference is given to men. Young
unmarried women are very likely to go into prostitution. Because
unmarried women by necessity are economically independent, they
are looked down upon, which further jeopardizes their choices
for marriage.

_____. "Women in Africa: Modernization Means More Dependence."
CENTER MAGAZINE 8 (May–June 1974): 60–67.

The author suggests that modernization will cause women to be
even more dependent on men. African urban women have greater
access to the benefits of modernization, since it is the most educated women who leave the villages. These women assume that
in the city they will find greater freedom from both arduous physical labor and restraints on behavior. However, unmarried women
in the cities have a much more difficult time than their rural
counterparts. They have little access to good jobs, and are cir-
cumscribed to petty trading, prostitution, illicit brewing, and the
like. Married urban women have greater economic and social
security, but at the price of greater dependence on their spouses.
If they have little or no education they are totally excluded from
decent jobs, partly because employers continue to prefer men.
Also, husbands fear what will happen if their wives go out and

work under the supervision of strange men. These married urban women find themselves in a double bind: they are no longer
on the land but are required to feed themselves and their children.
Moreover, the urban wives are generally cut off from collective
associations and activities with other women.

Ward, Barbara E. WOMEN IN THE NEW ASIA: THE CHANGING SOCIAL
ROLES OF MEN AND WOMEN IN SOUTH AND SOUTHEAST ASIA. Paris:
UNESCO, 1964. 529 p.

This monograph is based on research dealing with Burma, Ceylon,
India, Indonesia, Laos, Malaysia, Pakistan, Thailand, Vietnam,
Singapore, and the Philippines. The change from rural to urban
life brings with it a profound change in social roles. New employment patterns are important. Most migrant women who seek
jobs in the towns are in economic need, caused in part by the
migration itself. When the type of work which women get is examined, it is clear that a majority of gainfully employed women
in Asian cities have not entered into a new kind of employment,
despite the profound nature of the move.

Wilkinson, Thomas Oberson. THE URBANIZATION OF JAPANESE LABOR,
1868-1955. Amherst: University of Massachusetts Press, 1965. 243 p.

The author presents some statistics and data on urban women in
the Japanese labor force. He notes that the sex ratios of urban
employment are significantly higher than those of rural employment. The urban influence upon rates of female employment is
directly related to the size of the city. Generally, as the amount
of urban influences grows, there is a decrease in female employment. Urban sex ratios decreased between 1920 and 1950. Losses
in the number of women employees were primarily in the industrial
sector, but those losses were more than compensated in other
areas. Urban women began to approach the rate of rural females
only for those women under twenty and over sixty. Generally,
Japan's cities had been traditionally masculine, but between 1920
and 1950 there was a shift causing a decreasing predominance of
men, due more to changing male patterns than to changing female
patterns. As a result of this growing similarity between rural and
urban areas in terms of sex ratio and female employment, there
has been a decline in fertility in both areas. The urban environment generally influences the marriage age and the level of fertility.

Section V

WOMEN'S ROLES IN URBAN SOCIETY:

SOCIAL AND PSYCHOLOGICAL IMPLICATIONS

Included here are items dealing with women's attitudes towards urbanization, the process of female adjustment to city life, women's nonfamilial and non-employment urban activities, and women's role in urban politics and reform.

Abadan-Unat, Nermin. "Implications of Migration on Emancipation and Pseudo-Emancipation of Turkish Women." INTERNATIONAL MIGRATION REVIEW 11 (Spring 1977): 31-57.

Between 1955 and 1975 there has been a heavy external migration from Turkey to cities of Western Europe. At first the stream of migrants was predominantly male, but women too joined. By 1966 there was a great demand for Turkish women in the Federal German Republic. Turkish women were encouraged to migrate by family. These women, in the thousands, entered urban society without prior knowledge about the urban environment, knowing little about highly disciplined work hours or norms of industrial production. Migration thus created a chain reaction for women. This was true for workers as well as for unemployed females, who were at home. The movement of women into urban industrial work does not always bring with it signs of gradual emancipation. Employment is frequently viewed as temporary. There is a decrease in extended family involvement and an increase in nuclear family involvement creating changes in family patterns and women's roles. While this shift helps in stimulating positive feelings for girls' education, it is also associated with marital stress and breakup. Older daughters in a family, however, reap the least benefits from urbanization since they must take over many of the responsibilities previously held by the mother. Mobility and family fragmentation stimulate men to perform certain domestic responsibilities, but this ceases when the family returns to Turkey. Generally, the author sees urban migration as creating a model of "pseudo-emancipation" of women.

_____. SOCIAL CHANGE AND TURKISH WOMEN. Publications of the Faculty of Political Science of the University of Ankara, no. 171-153.

Ankara, Turkey: Ankara Universitese Basimevi, 1963. 36 p.

> The author notes that traditional behavior and expectations of
> women are stronger in the country than in the city. Some of
> the far-reaching effects of national reforms instituted by Ataturk
> could only be effective in an urban environment, where there is
> greater female literacy and contact with the media. Old patterns
> in the rural areas break down when greater contact is established
> with the urban areas, but outside of the cities little real laberali-
> zation of women's roles has occurred. The author provides some
> data on urban marriage rates. The author notes that the physical
> conditions of urban life, such as apartment dwellings, help create
> an atomistic family, with greater equality for women.

Bastide, Henri. "La Tâche des Femmes a La Campagne." ESPRIT 295
(1961): 938–45.

> This study of time use compares rural women with urban women.
> Because of rural fertility rates, the type of rural housing, and
> the lack of modern appliances, rural women spend more time
> working. The author notes that the only way farm women can
> lessen their work load is to migrate to the city.

Beard, Mary Ritter. WOMAN'S WORK IN MUNICIPALITIES. New York:
D. Appleton, 1915. 344 p. Reprint. New York: Arno Press, 1972.

> The author states four goals for this book: (1) to document the
> extent and variety of women's involvement in cities and towns;
> (2) to lay out women's own descriptions of the problems in Amer-
> ican cities; (3) to show the interrelationship of special problems
> with women in civic work and those becoming interested in it;
> and (4) to point out the general tendencies of women in contem-
> porary social work. The book provides information on women's
> involvement with education, public health, the "social evil,"
> recreation, race relations, housing, social service, correction,
> public safety, civic improvement, and government administration
> in the cities of the United States.

Bloom, Joseph D. "Migration and Psychopathology of Eskimo Women."
AMERICAN JOURNAL OF PSYCHIATRY 130 (April 1973): 446–49.

> Women comprise a greater percentage of young Eskimos who mi-
> grate from villages to cities and towns than men. These Eskimo
> women suffer greater psychological difficulty than male migrants
> or than those women who remain in the villages. Eskimo women
> migrate from the villages because of the low esteem in which
> they are held there. The crisis of migration and the high rate
> of failure in interpersonal relations in the city leads to increased
> and severe psychological problems.

Boulding, Elise. "Women as Role Models in Industrializing Societies: A Macro-System Model of Socialization for Civic Competence." In CROSS-NATIONAL FAMILY RESEARCH, edited by Marvin B. Sussman and Betty E. Cogswell, pp. 11-34. Leiden, Netherlands: E.J. Brill, 1972.

> Recency of urbanization is critical in determining the impact of city life on the roles of women. More recent urbanization has liberalized the status of women.

Brana-Shute, Rosemary. "Women, Clubs, and Politics: The Case of a Lower-Class Neighborhood in Paramaribo, Suriname." URBAN ANTHROPOLOGY 5 (Summer 1976): 157-85.

> Lower-class creole women, through kinship, residence, sexual division of labor, common adaptation to marginality, and ideology, are more cohesively bound together than are men. Social clubs arise out of female contacts. Within the clubs "cores" of friends form work and communication units that increase the flexibility and influence of the club and allow members access to urban services and resources unavailable to them as individuals. In Surinamese a kern is a local cell of a national political party. Women's clubs and associations may be important in local Suri-namese creole politics because women members share so many nonpolitical relationships.

Breckinridge, Sophonisba P. WOMEN IN THE TWENTIETH CENTURY: A STUDY OF THEIR POLITICAL, SOCIAL AND ECONOMIC ACTIVITIES. New York: McGraw-Hill, 1933. 364 p.

> This volume surveys the role of American women in politics and focuses on women in city government, as officeholders and activists. The author asserts that local urban politics has been the most promising arena for women's political expression. A listing of cities with women officeholders is included.

Bryce-Laporte, Roy Simon. "Urban Relocation and Family Adaptation in Puerto Rico: A Case Study in Urban Ethnography." In PEASANTS IN CITIES: THE ANTHROPOLOGY OF URBANIZATION, edited by William Mangin, pp. 85-97. Boston: Houghton-Mifflin Co., 1970.

> This is a study of a low-income housing project in San Juan, El Caserio. Of the residents, 40 percent had been transferred from nearby shanty-towns and 60 percent were from other slums and rural areas. While women enjoyed a preferred status when compared to their husbands, their freedom to act was circumscribed. Urbanization has brought opportunities and demands for employment by Puerto Rican women.

Chapin, F. Stuart, Jr. HUMAN ACTIVITY PATTERNS IN THE CITY: THINGS PEOPLE DO IN TIME AND IN SPACE. London: John Wiley and Sons, 1974. 272 p.

Those activities in the city which can be performed only away from home, like office and factory work, shopping, visiting, and certain recreational and leisure activities, are more available to men, who have a wider daily geographic radius than women.

Chinn, W.H. "Social Problems of Rapid Urbanization with Particular Reference to British Africa." In URBANIZATION IN AFRICAN SOCIAL CHANGE, pp. 90–101. Edinburgh: Edinburgh University, Centre of African Studies, 1963.

The economic independence of urban women leads to greater female authority within the family. Women have a greater self-interest in stabilizing the marital union. Urban life places greater strain and stress on women than on men.

Comhaire, Jean. INTRODUCTION TO THE URBAN PROBLEM IN TROPICAL AFRICA. Addis Ababa, Ethiopia: Haile Selassie I University, Department of Sociology, 1966. 58 p.

Emancipation of women is noted as a specifically urban phenomenon, although the author does not provide specific data on it.

Davis, Natalie Zemon. "City Women and Religious Change in Sixteenth Century France." In A SAMPLER OF WOMEN'S STUDIES, edited by Dorothy Gies McGuigan, pp. 17–45. Ann Arbor: University of Michigan Press, 1973.

The author describes the economic activities of French urban women in the age of the Reformation. Attention is also given to the social and religious roles played by these French women.

Dobbin, Christine E. URBAN LEADERSHIP IN WESTERN INDIA: POLITICS AND COMMUNITIES IN BOMBAY CITY, 1840–1885. London: Oxford University Press, 1972. 305 p.

Spurred on by the most urbanized groups in Bombay, by those people involved in commerce, and by the intellectuals, there was a major reform movement, which called for a vast expansion of female education and for a widow remarriage act.

Duval, Evelyn Mills, and Motz, Annabelle Bender. "Are Country Girls So Different?" RURAL SOCIOLOGY 10 (September 1945): 263–74.

The authors compared rural and urban girls in terms of social experiences and family adjustment. There were no significant differences in fourteen different areas, including happiness in childhood and adolescence, sources of information about sex, positive knowledge about sex, numbers of male and female friends, attitudes about married female employment, and values about children. The authors did, however, observe a number of significant differences. Rural girls generally lived under greater and firmer discipline. Urban girls were reported to be less consistent, and more urban than rural girls reported that they lived in an unhappy home. Urban girls smoked and drank more frequently than rural girls.

Fox, Greer Litton. "Some Determinants of Modernism among Women in Ankara, Turkey." JOURNAL OF MARRIAGE AND THE FAMILY 35 (August 1973): 520-29.

The author considers the idea of full participation of women in all areas of life to be an urban idea. One hypothesis being tested here is that the attitudes and behavior of women vary according to their rearing in rural as opposed to urban settings. This hypothesis is borne out by tables demonstrating the gross relationship between dependent variables and a number of urban generalizations. The author notes that labor force participation cannot be measured in Muslim countries, but must instead measure women's performances as wives. Other factors which are considered include education, age at marriage, media exposure, and the like.

Gans, Herbert J. "Effects of the Move from City to Suburb." In THE URBAN CONDITION, edited by Leonard J. Duhl, pp. 184-98. New York: Basic Books, 1963.

Women tend to be the unhappiest suburbanites. The author, however, asserts that this is not just a suburban phenomenon. The article researched both cosmopolitan women and working-class women.

_____. THE LEVITTOWNERS: WAYS OF LIFE AND POLITICS IN A NEW SUBURBAN COMMUNITY. New York: Pantheon Books, 1967. 474 p.

One central question to the study here was how did the move to suburbia affect peoples' lives? Among the few identifiable groups experiencing social isolation were women who did not work and who had come from a cohesive working-class community, where they were used to living and dealing with extended kin relations. The causes or roots of change came not from suburbia per se. The author asserts that what malaise existed in Levittown was found among the women. Among the women singled out were young women who had just had a child and had worked before coming to Levittown, working-class women who missed their kin, and women with poor marriages or where the husband was frequently absent.

Gulick, John, and Bowerman, Charles E. SOCIO-CULTURAL ADAPTATION OF NEWCOMERS TO CITIES IN THE PIEDMONT INDUSTRIAL CRESCENT

WITH AN APPENDIX ON SOCIAL STRATIFICATION. Chapel Hill: University of North Carolina, Institute for Research in Social Science, 1961. 95 p.

> This study examines migrants to Durham and Greensboro. Women generally exhibited greater attachment to both their present and former places of residence.

Gutman, Robert. "Population Mobility in the American Middle Class." In THE URBAN CONDITION: PEOPLE AND POLICY IN THE METROPOLIS, edited by Leonard J. Duhl, pp. 172-83. New York: Basic Books, 1963.

> This study of adjustment to suburban living provides some information and focus on the particular issues of women's adjustment. Working-class wives had more distant and cool relations with neighbors than did middle-class wives with greater education. Four types of women in the suburban setting who had adjustment problems were isolated: (1) downwardly mobile migrants; (2) the working-class wife who, although experiencing upward economic mobility was inexperienced at handling new situations; (3) emotionally expressive women of both the middle and working class; and (4) women with unusual interests and tastes.

Haavio-Mannila, Elina. "Sex Roles in Politics." In TOWARDS A SOCIOLOGY OF WOMEN, edited by Constantina Safilos-Rothschild, pp. 154-72. Lexington, Mass.: Xerox College Publishing, 1972.

> Modernization and urbanization have increased the political activities of both sexes and have decreased the differences between male political participation and female political participation. The author provides statistics on Finnish parliamentary and municipal elections from 1907 to 1968. She uses data from Helsinki, two small towns, and five rural communities. No differences were observed in rural and urban women's expectations of women's political interests, but urban women were more politically active than rural. Women were more likely to be elected to public office in the urban areas.

Harkess, Shirley J. "The Pursuit of an Ideal: Migration, Social Class, and Women's Roles in Bogota, Colombia." In FEMALE AND MALE IN LATIN AMERICA: ESSAYS, edited by Ann Pescatello, pp. 231-54. Pittsburgh: University of Pittsburgh Press, 1973.

> The author looks at two groups of female urban migrants: working-class women and poor women. The hypothesis is advanced that women who move to the city from traditional, provincial areas, adapt to urban life by modification of ideals, values, behavior, and action. The author notes that poor women who are recent migrants to the city bring traditional ideals with them, but quickly adopt new behavior. Later, with increased security about the urban environment, they are likely to return to the older values, actions, and behavior patterns.

Jahoda, Gustav. "Boys' Images of Marriage Partners and Girls' Self-Images in Ghana." SOCIOLOGUS 8, no. 2 (1958): 155-69.

> The author asks how sex role expectations change in an urban setting where the breakdown of traditional forms are most apparent. Social changes, synonymous with urbanization, have depressed the relative status of women, partly as a result of the greater advances made by men in education. In this study children were presented with a series of pictures of women, varying in type of dress, pigmentation, and the like. Sixty boys and sixty girls in six Accra schools were asked to choose which pictures they liked best. The children were in the early school years, those ages in which Western values were first formally introduced. The children reacted negatively to home background. The boys said they wanted to marry westernized women. The girls positively saw themselves as westernized. In adolescence, the author notes, there is a return to stressing the traditional. As the marriage age approaches, the girls realize that in marriage they will have to perform many traditional tasks.

Johnson, Allan Griswold. "Modernization and Social Change: Attitudes towards Women's Roles in Mexico City." Ph.D. Dissertation, University of Michigan, 1972.

> Mexico City wives were questioned about their attitudes on such subjects as dominance in marital decisions, involvement with kin, levels of media consumption, educational achievement, the process of urban migration, paid employment, and life in the urban environment. The researcher tested the hypothesis that such formal and measurable variables affect attitudes towards women's roles.

Keirn, Susan Middleton. "Voluntary Associations among Urban African Women." In CULTURE CHANGE IN CONTEMPORARY AFRICA, edited by Brian M. du Toit, pp. 25-40. Gainesville: University of Florida Press, 1970.

> Based on field research conducted in 1969 in Kwa Mashu, a South African town with a population of 100,000, this article treats the way in which African families adapt to the urban environment. The author identifies eight types of women's associations, each with its own distinctive function. The data indicates that these voluntary associations reflect an emerging structure, similar to a class structure. These women's associations will emerge as instruments by which urban African women distinguish status and prestige within their communities.

Leith-Ross, Sylvia. AFRICAN WOMEN: A STUDY OF THE IBO OF NIGERIA. London: Faber and Faber, 1939. 365 p.

This work is generally descriptive and anecdotal with some broad generalizations. The author describes women in a transitional town, Oweri Town. This was an urban farming community with a sharp division of labor between the sexes. The women went out every day to the farms and returned to the town at night. This town is contrasted to Port Harcourt, an entirely urban situation in which women are divorced from the natural environment. Urban women are in an entirely new sphere. There was an enormous increase in their leisure time due to the absence of gardening and farm work. While males in the cities far outnumber females, women too come alone to the city. Sometimes they came as long-distance traders. Some women rent plots of unused land from the township for gardens which they will plant for their own consumption. Other women leave the city twice a year to return to their husbands' homes to plant and then to harvest.

Leonard, Karen. "Women and Social Change in Modern India." FEMINIST STUDIES 3 (Spring-Summer 1976): 117-30.

This study of the Kaysath case attempts to locate indicators of political and social change for women. The Kaysath are an urbanized caste. The author presents seven variables useful in measuring changes both in women's behavior and in women's expectations: (1) patterns of naming women; (2) age at marriage; (3) amount and type of education; (4) employment outside the home, before and after marriage and motherhood; (5) the ratio of never-married women to all women; (6) marriage across caste and sub-caste lines; (7) marriage in or out of birth order.

Lerner, Daniel. THE PASSING OF TRADITIONAL SOCIETY: MODERNIZING THE MIDDLE EAST. Glencoe, Ill.: Free Press, 1958. 466 p.

Dealing with Turkey, the author notes that the liberating effects of modernization are most clearly evident among urban women, who have removed their veils. Among these women there has been a sharp increase in employment and a mushrooming of female literacy.

Little, Kenneth Lindsay. AFRICAN WOMEN IN TOWNS: AN ASPECT OF AFRICA'S SOCIAL REVOLUTION. London: Cambridge University Press, 1973. 242 p.

This study, based heavily on secondary sources, is perhaps the seminal work on urban women in Africa. The author notes that there is a good deal of ambiguity in the position of urban African women. The behavior of these women is "empirical" and the urban working woman is often more determined and committed to urban life than her male counterpart. Urbanization has encouraged women to create new forms of social alignments, and women tend to feel more positive about a permanent urban residence than many men. Women are, however, at an educational disadvantage with men in the city. Men seem to rely on older, traditional values as a form of moral support, because of the relatively open nature of the urban setting. This frequently stifles female competition. The urban situation poses a dilemma for women. Town life means that they have easier access to social and economic progress, partly because of the emergence of an urban family form which is nuclear. Yet, traditional attitudes about sex roles persist and they tend to undermine the success of the new family form and the woman's role in it. The state, or the society, has not yet provided other institutions of welfare, so in times of familial crisis, tradition wins out. The author asserts that, in the city, relations have become more complicated. This is less true in East Africa where there are fewer well-developed women's institutions, and where there is less equality or meeting ground between the sexes. Women come to the city to find independence. This motivation is common to a number of different classes of women. Most urban households are dependent on women's earning, especially the income of trading women, whose income is constant throughout the year, as opposed to the cyclical and sporadic nature of male urban employment. The urban economy is not based on a strict division of labor and while women are at a severe disadvantage because of lower educational levels, their earning power has led to greater independence and power. The author treats extensively voluntary associations among urban women, many of them growing out of the marketing situation. The voluntary associations help other women get started or help women in expanding their trading operations. In some cases women's associations have undertaken manufacturing, buying produce in bulk, and other such mutual aid projects. The women members have duties for the assistance of each other. Finally, the author analyzes the political life of these Sub-Saharan urban women. A number of the women's associations have banded together into national organizations which then function as political pressure groups.

_____. "Voluntary Associations and Social Mobility among West African Women." CANADIAN JOURNAL OF AFRICAN STUDIES 6, no. 2 (1972): 275-88.

Voluntary associations in urban West Africa help facilitate the upward social mobility of women.

_____. WEST AFRICAN URBANIZATION: A STUDY OF VOLUNTARY ASSOCIATIONS IN SOCIAL CHANGE. Cambridge: At the University Press, 1965. 179 p.

Many of the West African voluntary associations are exclusively female. Among these are associations of women traders, which help in the process of adapting the role of women to the urban environment, in both the technological and ideological spheres. They encourage and enable women to act in more individualistic patterns than the traditional system calls for, but which are critical to the urban economy. The actions of the voluntary associations allow them greater independence from their men. In the cities women need to redefine their role because urbanization has made the lives of certain types of women less secure than in traditional society. Because men outnumber women in cities, the voluntary associations serve as a critical link between men and women. Some voluntary associations serve the needs of the large numbers of urban prostitutes. In urban life the voluntary women's associations have filled a vacuum in social relations, caused by the erosion of parental and village/tribal authority.

Lopata, Helena Znaniecki. "Effects of Schooling on Social Contacts of Urban Women." AMERICAN JOURNAL OF SOCIOLOGY 79 (November 1973): 604-19.

This article is based on two sets of data: one dealing with 571 housewives and married working women; another one involving 301 widows over the age of fifty. The author attempts to discover the association between social relationships in the city and formal schooling for women. The author concludes that urbanization and industrialization have made formal education a major requirement for women's social involvement. The woman with less education is likely to have a greater degree of urban social isolation than the woman with more education. The variable of education is assessed to be the most important one in predicting the level of an urban woman's participation in society and her attitudes toward participation. The women included for study were all metropolitan, some suburban and some in the metropolitan center. The author generalizes that "modern urban life is increasingly breaking up the previously stable ethnic communities. . . . The rate of social change, especially the change experienced in the lives of women, is increasing the potential for social isolation on the part of those members of this sex who were trained into passive stances."

Mathewson, Marie Asnes. "Southern Ghanaian Women: Urban Residence and Migrational Cycles." Ph.D. Dissertation, University of Rochester, 1973.

This study attempts to locate and describe the types of resources, institutions, and networks available to urban women. Focusing on migrants to the city, the author attempts to isolate both urban and nonurban resources which women use in the process of adjusting to city life. The author notes that women migrants do interact with each other because of their shared values. The longer they remain in the city, the more extensive their urban contacts who can be called upon in various problem situations. These same women depend on nonurban resources in periods of crisis. In some situations they will leave the city and return to the tribal setting, as in the case of childbirth, severe illness, marital break-up, and debt.

Mayer, Philip. TOWNSMEN OR TRIBESMEN: CONSERVATISM AND THE PROCESS OF URBANIZATION IN A SOUTH AFRICAN CITY. Cape Town: Oxford University Press, 1961. 306 p.

This study surveys two Xhosa groups in East London: the Red Xhosa and the School Xhosa. The major concern here is the degree of resistance to urbanization and urban influences. A number of observations about women are made in the study. Women's activities, in the economic sphere, are midway between the urban and rural. Those women who are self-employed have an easy time maintaining their rural contacts. Domestic servants have much more difficulty and they adopt urban dress and manners much more quickly. For some women, success in the city enhances their rural prestige. There is a general agreement among both Red and School men and women that women have significantly greater freedom in the city. The city is the only place where women can own real property. Few of the women in East London are exclusively country-rooted, and even among the Red Xhosa, who are most resistant to urban influences, it is difficult for women to be immune to town contacts and interests. Women, in fact, seem to be more susceptible to urban society than the men. Of all of the migrants studied, the young women among the School Xhosa have the most positive preconceptions about urban life. In the country, both Red and School parents expect that their sons will go to town, at some point, but not their daughters. Among the Red any girl who goes to town for anything but a short visit jeopardizes her chances for marriage, yet this is not compensated for by chances of urban marriage. School women have greater and wider economic opportunities than Red women. The author notes that except for factory work, women's employment serves to encourage townlike independent behavior and attitudes. Women rarely have the same "incapsulating social circle" that the male migrants have.

Meillassoux, Claude. URBANIZATION OF AN AFRICAN COMMUNITY: VOLUNTARY ASSOCIATIONS IN BAMAKO. Seattle: University of Washington Press, 1968. 165 p.

Based on research carried out in Mali in 1962 and 1963 the author studied popular urban culture and in particular urban clubs. The author notes that urbanization and modernization have brought about a rapid emancipation of women's roles. In the cities, married women cannot make money selling produce raised by their husbands, so they flock to women's mutual aid societies to provide alternate sources of income.

Metge, Alice Joan. A NEW MAORI MIGRATION: RURAL AND URBAN RELATIONS IN NORTHERN NEW ZEALAND. London: Athlone Press, 1964. 299 p.

> In contrast to the rural areas, women in Auckland are much more politically active and are frequently elected to public office. There is an expansion of the range of women's activities. Auckland has an equal distribution of the sexes.

Mitchell, J. Clyde. "The Woman's Place in African Advancement." OPTIMA 9 (September 1959): 124–31.

> The author first sets forth the status of women in traditional-tribal society and then contrasts it with city living. Women seem to have more problems in adjustment to urban life, and most African women are dissatisfied with their urban role, even though certain traditional and "irksome" tasks are obviated by the urban condition. The author discusses the changes in the bridewealth in the city and notes that the new urban environment calls for new definitions of women's roles. Most African women were brought up in a tribal setting and are unprepared to deal with the changes in family structure. Where the urban husband and wife are from different tribes, they see themselves as representatives of two different kin groups sharing the same domestic establishment.

Murickan, J. "Women in Kerala: Changing Socio-Economic Status and Self-Image." In WOMEN IN CONTEMPORARY INDIA: TRADITIONAL IMAGES AND CHANGING ROLES, edited by Alfred de Souza, pp. 73–95. Delhi: Manohar, 1975.

> The author describes the impact of urbanization and education on the attitudes, values, and behavior of younger generation Kerala women. While the author believes that education is the key variable in greater female self-esteem, the urban woman is far ahead of her rural counterpart. The author sees this in a number of areas. He found, for example, that a greater gap in religious practices exists between urban mothers and their more educated daughters than among rural mothers and their daughters.

Oeser, Lynn. HOHOLA: THE SIGNIFICANCE OF SOCIAL NETWORKS IN URBAN ADAPTATION OF WOMEN IN PAPUA-NEW GUINEA'S FIRST LOW-COST HOUSING ESTATE. New Guinea Research Bulletin, no. 29. Canberra: Australian National University, New Guinea Research Unit, 1969. 120 p.

> This monograph notes that the number of associations a woman maintains with others is related to her ability to cope with daily tasks. The more complex her social network, the better she will be able to cope. Urbanization does not sever a woman's links with tradition or with the rural setting. In attitude towards contraception, there is a clear urban-rural difference; urban women are much more positive and aware of birth control.

Parkin, David. NEIGHBOURS AND NATIONALS IN AN AFRICAN CITY WARD. London: Routledge and Kegan Paul, 1969. 228 p.

This is a study of Kenyans who moved to Kampala East, in Uganda. A significant number of the women are really only partly urbanized, since they spend up to half the year back in the rural area. When they are in the city, however, the neighborhood unit is a much more significant factor in their lives than in the men's.

Pellow, Deborah. "Women of Accra: A Study of Options." Ph.D. Dissertation, Northwestern University, 1974.

This dissertation begins with a review of the literature on urban West African women. In much of the analysis of the field, women are portrayed as enjoying a good deal of power in their modernizing society and as having a wider variety of educational and employment opportunities. Yet these women, and men, come to the cities from traditional societies which equate status with such factors as age, sex, and family origins. The values of this system are carried into the city with the migrants. The study proposes that women do not in fact enjoy new alternatives based on certain urban advantages. Using a randomly selected cross-section of inner-city Accra women, the author tests this proposition. In Accra women have the disadvantages of both the old and the new woman. They are always pushed into the same sexually defined roles, yet the advantages of urban life are closed off to them because they are women. They, however, no longer have the defenses of traditional society which protected women within their kin unit and tribe in the rural areas. Western attitudes and practices toward women have not displaced old values but neither have they been well incorporated into general practices. The author isolates five traditional attitudes which have remained in the city: traditional attitudes towards reciprocity, polygyny, seniority, liability, and fatalism. These attitudes are in fact reinforced by the new institutions. The author stresses that structural changes due to urbanization are irrelevant to women's lives.

Pivar, David J. PURITY CRUSADE: SEXUAL MORALITY AND SOCIAL CONTROL: 1868-1900. Westport, Conn.: Greenwood Press, 1973. 308 p.

This study of morality reform in the United States is primarily urban and the author notes that women played a very important role here. These urban women launched crusades involving a number of women's issues, including prostitution and white slavery. The author believes that many of these reform movements helped set the scene for later birth control agitation.

Pons, Valdo. STANLEYVILLE: AN AFRICAN URBAN COMMUNITY UNDER BELGIAN ADMINISTRATION. London: Oxford University Press, 1969. 356 p.

Urban life has largely freed women of certain limitations and pressures of traditional life, but they still lag far behind men in economic status, occupational level, and educational attainment. Most women continue to be dependent on their menfolk. Urban feminine roles come to be defined in more strictly sexual and domestic terms than in the rural, tribal setting of their youth.

Powdermaker, Hortense. COPPER TOWN: CHANGING AFRICA: THE HUMAN SITUATION ON THE RHODESIAN COPPERBELT. New York: Harper and Row, 1962. 391 p. Reprint. Westport, Conn.: Greenwood Press, 1973.

The author first presents the rural tribal setting in which men and women had different, though integrated, roles. Men were clearly in a superior position. In agriculture, women were the hoers, while men wielded the axe. There were separate rituals for men and women as well as separate social spheres. In town men and women no longer had communal economic tasks. Men and women entered the modern urban world at different rates, with women's lives and work generally confined to home. This is a drastic change for African women who entered urban society from a situation where they had had a female communal group with economic, social, and ritual functions. Generally women seemed to be pleased with town life, but not too comfortable. In the town there was increased conflict with their husbands. Most conflicts were over money, a new subject of controversy, since in the tribe they had been economic partners. Another new area of conflict was between the duties and responsibilities of the new conjugal family and the traditional extended family. The women studied demonstrated no change in the desired number of children, although the author projected that in the future there would be a change, bringing with it a decline in fertility. The author also found a weakening of the strength of traditional upbringing for girls. There were new forms of family behavior, although traditions lingered on. The new female expectations were clear, although opportunities for actualizing them were limited. The absence of strong lineage group ties added to female insecurity. The author concludes, "In the emergence of the patriarchally-oriented conjugal family and the weakening of the extended lineage unit, the men gained more economic and psychologic independence than did the women. The break from the past, the finding of a new identity were far more difficult for them."

Preston-Whyte, E.M. "The Adaptation of Rural-Born Female Domestic Servants to Town Life." In FOCUS ON CITIES: PROCEEDINGS OF A CONFERENCE ORGANISED BY THE INSTITUTE FOR SOCIAL RESEARCH AT THE UNIVERSITY OF NATAL, DURBAN, 8-12 JULY, 1968, edited by H.L. Watts, pp. 271-81. Durban, South Africa: Institute for Social Research, University of Natal, 1970.

Migrant African women maintain extensive rural and urban ties. The author asks how these ties facilitate the process of integration and adaptation to city life and what is the effect of close contact with employers for migrant women. The research found that kin ties predominate even in the city. Often urban kin provide the link into the city and the job. This same pattern and the continued dependence on kin is not manifested by male servants, the "house boys." For women, kinship in town functions differently than it did in the rural setting.

Probbhu, Pandhari Nath. "Bombay: A Study on the Social Effects of Urbanization on Industrial Workers Migrating from Rural Areas to the City of Bombay." In THE SOCIAL IMPLICATIONS OF INDUSTRIALIZATION AND URBANIZATION: FIVE STUDIES IN ASIA, edited by UNESCO, Research Centre on Social and Economic Development in Southern Asia, pp. 50–106. Calcutta: UNESCO, 1956.

The author discerns an expansion of women's freedom in the urban setting. There is a clear trend toward urban-rural differences in attitudes on such questions as marriage age, education of women, and arranged versus consensual marriages.

Rosen, Bernard, and La Raia, Anita L. "Modernity in Women: An Index of Social Change in Brazil." JOURNAL OF MARRIAGE AND THE FAMILY 34 (May 1972): 353–60.

The authors studied by factor analysis 816 married fertile women in terms of their attitudes and behavior concerning the role of women as wives and mothers. Women in industrial cities have greater voice in family decision making, have a better opinion of all women, and urge greater independence in their children. These women participate more actively in the community than do rural women or women in nonindustrial communities. The authors see industrialism as a more significant factor than urbanization.

Schwarzweller, Harry K.; Brown, James S.; and Mangalam, J.J. MOUNTAIN FAMILIES IN TRANSITION: A CASE STUDY OF APPALACHIAN MIGRANTS. University Park: Pennsylvania State University Press, 1971. 300 p.

This is a follow-up study of a 1942 project of an Appalachian town, given the pseudonym Beech Creek, Kentucky. In the outmigration from Beech Creek to the urban areas, the authors traced the changes in the stem family. The authors assert that women urban migrants seemed to be more satisfied with urban life than men, yet they demonstrated a higher level of anxiety than did the men. Women were less likely to yearn for home and were more at ease with the urban situation. Women had a discontinuity in their social role and the authors assert that this caused a frustration in their social interactions, which was complicated by the actualities of urban life.

Steckert, Ellen. "Focus for Conflict: Southern Mountain Medical Beliefs in Detroit." JOURNAL OF AMERICAN FOLKLORE 83 (April-June 1970): 115-56.

> This was a study of indigent southern mountain women in Detroit, and the author was interested in finding out why they did not seek or absorb medical information. In the first generation these women acquired little or no prenatal and postnatal care, few experienced hospital births. This pattern had been brought to the city from rural life. Among the explanations for this maternity behavior, the author notes (1) a glorification of the past; (2) the difficulty of movement within the city, especially for the migrants; (3) the role of women in the traditional setting as the dispensers of medical lore; (4) negative attitudes about welfare; (5) fear of doctors and the need for personal attention; and finally, (5) a tradition of self-diagnosis which accompanied a persistence of folk medicine. In subsequent generations the author found a decline in breast feeding, even though the women all believed that it was best. The author notes that some of the traditional birth practices and beliefs could be perpetuated in a hospital setting, others could not.

Stone, Gregory P. "City Shoppers and Urban Identification: Observations on the Social Psychology of City Life." AMERICAN JOURNAL OF SOCIOLOGY 40 (July 1954): 36-45.

> In this study of Chicago housewives, the author identifies four types of shoppers: economic, personalizing, ethical, and apathetic. Each type of shopper was characterized by a specific set of social characteristics which reflected her position in the urban social structure. The data was based on responses from 150 women who were administered a schedule about shopping. Generally, women derived a positive identification with urban life through shopping.

Suttles, Gerald D. THE SOCIAL ORDER OF THE SLUM: ETHNICITY AND TERRITORY IN THE INNER CITY. Chicago: University of Chicago Press, 1968. 243 p.

> One important component of this study is the discussion of sex segregation, a phenomenon which cuts across age lines. Girls either remained in their place or they ran the risk of ruining their reputation. This was especially true of the Italians, and less true among the blacks.

Szalai, Alexander. "The Situation of Women in Light of Contemporary Time-Budget Research." In WORLD CONFERENCE OF THE INTERNATIONAL WOMEN'S YEAR: CONFERENCE BACKGROUND PAPER. Presented in Mexico City, 19 June-2 July, 1975. Mimeograph.

Based on multinational comparative time-budget studies, involving fifteen sample surveys in a dozen countries, mostly focusing on medium-sized cities, the article noted that on the average women in the labor force continue to have a tremendous burden of housework. This is particularly striking when their domestic work is compared to that of men. The author asserts that technology will not change the situation, and only attitudinal reform will help. The author believes that women prefer traditional activities, and therefore they bear part of the blame, since they have adapted to and accepted the uneven distribution of labor.

Thomas, Norman E. "Functions of Religious Institutions in the Adjustment of African Women to Life in a Rhodesian Township." In FOCUS ON CITIES: PROCEEDINGS OF A CONFERENCE ORGANISED BY THE INSTITUTE FOR SOCIAL RESEARCH AT THE UNIVERSITY OF NATAL, DURBAN, 8-12 JULY, 1968, edited by H.L. Watts, pp. 282-290. Durban, South Africa: Institute for Social Research, University of Natal, 1970.

Based on 5 percent random cluster sample of women's clubs in Sakubva township of Umtale, the article noted that the strength of church women's groups can be explained by social factors including the provision of services and the absence of other stronger associations competing for urban women's loyalties. The author also found functional reasons for these clubs which were peculiarly urban. These clubs provided social life, status, recognition, and security for women in a new, and often hostile, urban environment.

Traver, James D. "Gradients of Urban Influence on the Educational, Employment, and Fertility Patterns of Women." RURAL SOCIOLOGY 34 (September 1969): 356-67.

The question here was whether significant rural-urban differences among certain characteristics still affect women in the 1960s. The findings were that fertility of women in 208 counties has increased directly with the increase away from the nearest metropolitan center. Formal education and the proportion of women in gainful employment declined as the distance increased. The number of children born per 1,000 women, ever-married, between thirty-five and forty-four, declined as the population size of the Standard Metropolitan Statistical Area increased. The proportion of women employed and the proportion of those with more than twelve years of education increased directly with population size in the metropolitan area.

Wilson, Monica, and Mabeje, Archie. LANGA: A STUDY OF SOCIAL GROUPS IN AN AFRICAN TOWNSHIP. London: Oxford University Press, 1963. 190 p.

This study of a South African urban area notes that town life brings with it a desire for fewer children, but traditional African methods for spacing of children are used to bring this about. Town life also brings greater educational opportunities for women, which is related to employment opportunities. Town life also causes a more equitable relationship between husband and wife.

Windham, Gerald O. "Formal Participation of Migrant Housewives in an Urban Community." SOCIOLOGY AND SOCIAL RESEARCH 47 (January 1963): 201-9.

Differences in social participation patterns among various types of housewives are pointed out and related to length of urban residence. The longer-time residents of Pittsburgh had more extensive social contacts than more recent arrivals.

Section VI

VIEWS OF URBAN WOMEN

This brief section contains references to works which assess how men, both rural and urban, view the urban woman and how they believe urbanization has affected women's behavior.

Gutkind, Peter Claus Wolfgang. URBAN ANTHROPOLOGY: PERSPECTIVES ON 'THIRD WORLD' URBANISATION AND URBANISM. Assen, Netherlands: Van Gorcum, 1974. 270 p.

> Among the observations in this interpretive volume, the author notes that most young men in the city will return to the rural village to find a wife. They will be reluctant to marry "town women" who have a reputation for free living and independent behavior.

Mayer, Philip. TOWNSMEN OR TRIBESMEN: CONSERVATISM AND THE PROCESS OF URBANIZATION IN A SOUTH AFRICAN CITY. Cape Town: Oxford University Press, 1961. 306 p.

> This study of two groups of Xhosa, Red and School, in East London notes that there is a consensus that urban women enjoy a great deal of freedom. Most rural parents of both the Red and School groups expect that their sons will go to the city, but if a daughter leaves the village for anything longer than a brief visit, she will be ostracized. In fact, a young woman who has lived in the city jeopardizes her chances for marriage, in both the rural area and in the town. The move to the city is, however, considered acceptable for some types of women: widows, mature unmarried women, unmarriageable women, and unwed mothers.

Pescatello, Ann. "The Brazileira: Images and Realities in Writings of Machado de Assis and Jorge Amado." In FEMALE AND MALE IN LATIN AMERICA, edited by Ann Pescatello, pp. 29-55. Pittsburgh: University of Pittsburgh Press, 1973.

One of the consistent features in the novels studied here was the portrayal of the young rural woman who comes to the city and drifts into prostitution or some kind of menial position. In these novels rural women seem to be less conscious of class distinctions than urban women. Most of the novels do not portray any signif-icant changes in the character of women with urban migration and urbanization.

_____. POWER AND PAWN: THE FEMALE IN IBERIAN FAMILIES, SOCI-ETIES, AND CULTURES. Westport, Conn.: Greenwood Press, 1976. 281 p.

The growth of cities in the Iberian world has threatened the tra-ditional codes of law, as codified in the thirteenth century, and traditional practices. The "cult of womanhood" reached its ob-sessive height as these societies in both Europe and Latin America were undergoing the process of urbanization.

Provencher, Ronald. TWO MALAY WORLDS: INTERACTION IN URBAN AND RURAL SETTINGS. Berkeley: Center for South and Southeast Asia Studies, University of California, 1971. 211 p.

Urban parents are worried about the influences of city life on their adolescent daughters. The traditional seclusion for teenage girls is difficult to maintain in the city, so these girls are often sent back to the countryside.

Safilios-Rothschild, Constantina. "Honor Crimes in Contemporary Greece." In her TOWARDS A SOCIOLOGY OF WOMEN, pp. 84-95. Lexington, Mass.: Xerox College Publishing, 1972.

The author culled reports of honor crimes from the Athenian news-papers for a three-year period. Most of the honor crimes com-mitted in the city were perpetrated by rural men who came to the city purposely seeking out the victim. The assumption is that women in the city are less able to defend themselves and their honor.

Simic, Andrei. THE PEASANT URBANITES: A STUDY OF RURAL-URBAN MOBILITY IN SERBIA. New York: Seminar Press, 1973. 180 p.

One important area of ambivalence and distrust in the city con-cerns urban women. Peasant men frequently prefer to choose a bride from among the young girls still in the village, be it their own village of origin or the villages surrounding Belgrade.

Van Allen, Judith. "African Women, 'Modernization,' and National Liber-ation." In WOMEN: A COMPARATIVE STUDY, edited by Lynne B. Iglitzen and Ruth Ross, pp. 25-54. Santa Barbara, Calif.: Clio Books, 1976.

African urban men clearly prefer to marry women from the village over city women. A man may live with a city woman for an extended period of time while he is saving his money to purchase a bridewealth for a girl in the village. Because town women are by necessity independent, they are generally thought of as free living and involved in a disreputable life-style. These women, however, provide an important service for urban men. They provide a refuge from urban anonymity and thereby help the urban economy which needs male workers who will remain in the city.

Wipper, Audrey. "African Women, Fashion, and Scapegoating." CANADIAN JOURNAL OF AFRICAN STUDIES 6, no. 2 (1972): 329-49.

African women and their styles of clothing are being used as symbols of aggression engendered by rapid and fundamental social change. Urban life is seen as disruptive to the family unit, and the highly visible urban woman is held up as the cause and source of family disintegration. Urban women are identified with modern fashion which in turn is held up as a threat to the ideal of the subservient hardworking woman. Men do not understand women's urban occupations. Thus urban women are scapegoated. They are not, however, in a position from which they can defend themselves against these attacks.

Appendix A
SELECTED BIBLIOGRAPHY

These books are recommended for the small library or for personal reference.

ANTHROPOLOGICAL QUARTERLY 49 (January 1976): entire issue.
 Special issue on women and culture change, including a number
 of articles on women and urbanization.

Bascom, William R., and Herskovits, Melville J. CONTINUITY AND
CHANGE IN AFRICAN CULTURES. Chicago: University of Chicago Press,
1959. 309 p.

Boserup, Ester. WOMEN'S ROLE IN ECONOMIC DEVELOPMENT. London:
George Allen and Unwin, 1970. 283 p.

Bott, Elizabeth. FAMILY AND SOCIAL NETWORK: ROLES, NORMS, AND
EXTERNAL RELATIONSHIPS IN ORDINARY URBAN FAMILIES. London:
Tavistock, 1957. 252 p.

Caldwell, John Charles. AFRICAN RURAL-URBAN MIGRATION: THE
MOVEMENT TO GHANA'S TOWNS. Canberra: Australian National University Press, 1969. 258 p.

_____. POPULATION GROWTH AND FAMILY CHANGE IN AFRICA: THE
NEW URBAN ELITE IN GHANA. Canberra: Australian National University
Press, 1968. 222 p.

CANADIAN JOURNAL OF AFRICAN STUDIES 6, no. 2 (1972): entire
issue.
 Special issue on African urban society.

Cohen, Abner. CUSTOM AND POLITICS IN URBAN AFRICA: A STUDY

OF HAUSA MIGRANTS IN YORUBA TOWNS. London: Routledge and Kegan Paul, 1969. 252 p.

Cornelius, Wayne A., and Trueblood, Felicity, eds. LATIN AMERICAN URBAN RESEARCH: ANTHROPOLOGICAL PERSPECTIVES ON LATIN AMERICAN URBANIZATION, vol. 4. Beverly Hills, Calif.: Sage Publications, 1974.

de Souza, Alfred, ed. WOMEN IN CONTEMPORARY INDIA: TRADITIONAL IMAGES AND CHANGING ROLES. Delhi: Manohar, 1975. 264 p.

Dyos, Harold James, and Wolff, Michael, eds. THE VICTORIAN CITY: IMAGE AND REALITIES. 2 vols. London: Routledge and Kegan Paul, 1973. 957 p.

González, Nancy L. Solien. BLACK CARIB HOUSEHOLD STRUCTURE: A STUDY OF MIGRATION AND MODERNIZATION. Seattle: University of Washington Press, 1969. 163 p.

Gutkind, Peter Claus Wolfgang. URBAN ANTHROPOLOGY: PERSPECTIVES ON 'THIRD WORLD' URBANISATION AND URBANISM. Assen, Netherlands: Van Gorcum, 1974. 270 p.

Hauser, Philip Morris. HANDBOOK FOR SOCIAL RESEARCH IN URBAN AREAS. Paris: UNESCO, 1965. 214 p.

Humphreys, Alexander Jeremiah. NEW DUBLINERS: URBANIZATION AND THE IRISH FAMILY. London: Routledge and Kegan Paul, 1966. 295 p.

Krapf-Askari, Eva. YORUBA TOWNS AND CITIES: AN ENQUIRY INTO THE NATURE OF URBAN SOCIAL PHENOMENA. Oxford: Clarendon Press, 1969. 195 p.

Little, Kenneth Lindsay. AFRICAN WOMEN IN TOWNS: AN ASPECT OF AFRICA'S SOCIAL REVOLUTION. London: Cambridge University Press, 1973. 242 p.

_____. URBANIZATION AS A SOCIAL PROCESS: AN ESSAY ON MOVEMENT AND CHANGE IN CONTEMPORARY AFRICA. London: Routledge and Kegan Paul, 1974. 153 p.

_____. WEST AFRICAN URBANIZATION: A STUDY OF VOLUNTARY ASSOCIATIONS IN SOCIAL CHANGE. Cambridge: At the University Press, 1965. 179 p.

Lopata, Helena Z[naniecki]. WIDOWHOOD IN AN AMERICAN CITY. Cambridge: Shenkman, 1973. 360 p.

Marris, Peter. AFRICAN CITY LIFE. Kampala, Uganda: Transition Books, 1967. 260 p.

_____. FAMILY AND SOCIAL CHANGE IN AN AFRICAN CITY: A STUDY OF REHOUSING IN LAGOS. London: Routledge and Kegan Paul, 1962. 180 p.

Mayer, Philip. TOWNSMEN OR TRIBESMEN: CONSERVATISM AND THE PROCESS OF URBANIZATION IN A SOUTH AFRICAN CITY. Cape Town: Oxford University Press, 1961. 306 p.

Miner, Horace, ed. THE CITY IN MODERN AFRICA. New York: Praeger, 1967. 364 p.

Pescatello, Ann, ed. FEMALE AND MALE IN LATIN AMERICA: ESSAYS. Pittsburgh: University of Pittsburgh Press, 1973. 342 p.

Phillips, Arthur, ed. SURVEY OF AFRICAN MARRIAGE AND FAMILY LIFE. London: Oxford University Press, 1953. 462 p.

Powdermaker, Hortense. COPPER TOWN: CHANGING AFRICA: THE HUMAN SITUATIONS ON THE RHODESIAN COPPERBELT. New York: Harper and Row, 1962. 391 p. Reprint. Westport, Conn.: Greenwood Press, 1973.

Ross, Aileen D. THE HINDU FAMILY IN ITS URBAN SETTING. Toronto: University of Toronto Press, 1967. 325 p.

Safilios-Rothschild, Constantina, ed. TOWARDS A SOCIOLOGY OF WOMEN. Lexington, Mass.: Xerox College Publishing, 1972. 406 p.

Schwarzweller, Harry K.; Brown, James S.; and Mangalam, J.J. MOUNTAIN FAMILIES IN TRANSITION: A CASE STUDY OF APPALACHIAN MIGRANTS. University Park: Pennsylvania State University Press, 1971. 300 p.

Southall, Aidan, ed. SOCIAL CHANGE IN MODERN AFRICA. London: Oxford University Press, 1961. 337 p.

Tinker, Irene; Bromsen, Michéle Bo; and Buvinić, Mayra, eds. WOMEN AND WORLD DEVELOPMENT. New York: Praeger, 1976. 240 p.

Selected Bibliography

URBANIZATION IN AFRICAN SOCIAL CHANGE. Edinburgh: Edinburgh University, Centre of African Studies, 1963. 206 p.

Ward, Barbara E. WOMEN IN THE NEW ASIA: THE CHANGING SOCIAL ROLES OF MEN AND WOMEN IN SOUTH AND SOUTHEAST ASIA. Paris: UNESCO, 1964. 529 p.

Appendix B

ABSTRACTS AND INDEXES

AMERICAN DOCTORAL DISSERTATIONS. Ann Arbor, Mich.: Association of Research Libraries. 1955/56-- . Annual.

COMPREHENSIVE DISSERTATION INDEX (1861-1972). Ann Arbor, Mich.: Xerox University Microfilms. Annual updates.

DISSERTATION ABSTRACTS INTERNATIONAL. Ann Arbor, Mich.: University Microfilms. 1938-- . Monthly.

POPULATION INDEX. Princeton, N.J.: Population Association of America. 1935-- . Quarterly.

PUBLIC AFFAIRS INFORMATION SERVICE. New York: Public Affairs Information Service. 1915-- . Weekly.

SAGE URBAN STUDIES ABSTRACTS. Beverly Hills, Calif.: Sage Publications. 1973-- . Quarterly.

SOCIAL SCIENCES CITATION INDEX. Philadelphia: Institute for Scientific Information. 1973-- . Triannual.

SOCIAL SCIENCES INDEX. New York: Wilson. 1974. Quarterly.

SOCIOLOGICAL ABSTRACTS. New York: Sociological Abstracts. 1952-- . Irregular.

WOMEN'S STUDIES ABSTRACTS. Rush, N.Y.: 1972-- . Quarterly.

Appendix C
PERIODICALS WITH CONTENT RELEVANT TO WOMEN AND URBAN SOCIETY

AFRICA. London: Oxford University Press. 1928-- . Quarterly.

AFRICAN STUDIES. Johannesburg: Witwatersrand University Press. 1942-- . Quarterly.

AFRICAN WOMEN. London: Department of Education in Tropical Areas, University of London Institute of Education. 1954-- . Semiannual.

AMERICAN ANTHROPOLOGIST. Menasha, Wis.: American Anthropological Association. 1898-- . Irregular.

AMERICAN JOURNAL OF SOCIOLOGY. Chicago: University of Chicago Press. 1895-- . Bimonthly.

AMERICAN SOCIOLOGICAL REVIEW. Menasha, Wis.: American Sociological Association. 1936-- . Bimonthly.

ANTHROPOLOGICAL QUARTERLY. Washington, D.C.: Catholic University of America Press. 1928-- .

CANADIAN JOURNAL OF AFRICAN STUDIES. Montreal: Loyola College. 1966-- . Triannual.

COMPARATIVE STUDIES IN SOCIETY AND HISTORY. The Hague, Netherlands: Mouton. 1958-- . Quarterly.

DEMOGRAPHY. Chicago: Population Association of America. 1964-- . Quarterly.

ECONOMIC DEVELOPMENT AND CULTURAL CHANGE. Chicago: University of Chicago, Research Center in Economic Development and Cultural Change. 1952-- . Irregular.

ETHNOLOGY. Pittsburgh: University of Pittsburgh. 1962-- . Quarterly.

HUMAN ORGANIZATION. New York: Society for Applied Anthropology. 1941-- . Quarterly.

HUMAN RELATIONS. London: Tavistock Publications. 1947-- . Quarterly.

INDIAN JOURNAL OF SOCIAL WORK. Bombay: The Sir Dorabji Tata Graduate School of Social Work. 1940-- . Quarterly.

INTERNATIONAL MIGRATION REVIEW. Staten Island, N.Y.: Center for Migration Studies. 1967-- . Triennial.

JOURNAL OF DEVELOPING AREAS. Macomb: Western Illinois University Press. 1966-- . Quarterly.

JOURNAL OF INTERDISCIPLINARY HISTORY. Cambridge, Mass.: M.I.T. Press. 1970-- . Quarterly.

JOURNAL OF MARRIAGE AND THE FAMILY. Menasha, Wis.: National Council on Family Relations. 1939-- . Quarterly.

JOURNAL OF REPRODUCTION AND FERTILITY. Oxford: Blackwell Scientific Publications. 1960-- . Bimonthly.

JOURNAL OF SOCIAL HISTORY. Berkeley and Los Angeles: University of California Press. 1967-- . Quarterly.

JOURNAL OF SOCIAL ISSUES. New York: Society for the Psychological Study of Social Issues. 1945-- . Quarterly.

MILBANK MEMORIAL FUND QUARTERLY. New York: Milbank Memorial Fund. 1923-- .

POPULATION STUDIES. Cambridge, Engl.: Population Investigation Committee, at the University Press. 1947-- . Quarterly.

RHODES-LIVINGSTON JOURNAL. Capetown: Oxford University Press. 1944-- . Irregular.

RURAL SOCIOLOGY. Baton Rouge, La.: American Sociological Society. 1936-- . Quarterly.

SOCIAL AND ECONOMIC STUDIES. Mona, Jamaica: Institute of Social and Economic Research, University College of the West Indies. 1953-- . Irregular.

SOCIAL FORCES. Chapel Hill: University of North Carolina Press. 1922-- . Quarterly.

SOCIOLOGICAL QUARTERLY. Carbondale, Ill.: Southern Illinois University Press. 1960-- .

SOCIOLOGICAL REVIEW. Keele, Engl.: University of Keele, 1953-- . Irregular.

SOCIOLOGICAL SYMPOSIUM. Bowling Green: Western Kentucky University. 1968-- . Biannual.

SOCIOLOGY AND SOCIAL RESEARCH. Los Angeles: University of Southern California. 1921-- . Bimonthly.

SOUTHWESTERN JOURNAL OF ANTHROPOLOGY. Albuquerque: University of New Mexico. 1945-- . Quarterly.

URBAN ANTHROPOLOGY. Brockport, N.Y.: SUNY-Brockport. 1972-- . Semiannual.

AUTHOR INDEX

Indexed here are all authors, editors, and compilers, as well as organizations acting as corporate authors. Coauthors are listed individually. This index is alphabetized letter by letter. Numbers refer to page numbers.

Author Index

Church, Roy A. 2, 18
Clemmer, Myrtle M. 44
Clignet, Remi 18-19,
Cochran, Lillian T. 54-55
Cogswell, Betty E. 93
Cohen, Abner 2, 76-77, 113-14
Collver, Andrew O. 55, 77
Comhaire, Jean L. 20, 94
Cornelius, Wayne A. 29, 114

D

Darlow, Mary 2-3
Davis, Natalie Zemon 94
De Abuquerque, Klaus 55-56
de Assis, Machado 109-10
Denich, Bette S. 20
de Souze, Alfred 48, 102, 114
Djamour, Judith 20
Dobbin, Christine E. 94
Dore, Ronald Philip 20-21
Dubey, Dinesh Chandra 56
Ducoff, Louis J. 6
Duhl, Leonard J. 96
Duncan, Otis Dudley 56
du Toit, Brian M. 97
Duval, Evelyn Mills 94-95
Duza, Mohammed Badrud 56
Dyos, Harold James 47-48, 51, 114

E

Eames, Edwin 21
Economic Commission for Africa 77-78
Economic Commission for Latin America 78
Einsiedel, Luz 21

F

Farley, Reynolds 56-57
Feldman, Kerry D. 57
Ferraro, Gary P. 21
Folger, John 3
Foner, N. 78-79
Fox, Greer Litton 95
Fraenkel, Merran 79
Frazier, E. Franklin p. xi, 21, 22

G

Gadgil, Dhananjaya Ramchandra 79
Gans, Herbert J. 95
Gardner, Bruce 57
Gartley, Jaco E. 22
Gerken, Egbert 22
Gibson, Jeffry Royle 3
Goldberg, David 57-58
Goldstein, Sideny 58
González, Nancy L. Solien 3-4, 23, 114
Good, Dorothy 58
Goodarzi, Abalhassan Moazami 58-59
Gore, Madhave Sadashiv 4, 23
Gould, Ketayuan H. 59
Graves, Nancy Beatrice 23-24
Gugler, Josef 4
Gulati, Subhash Chander 24
Gulick, John 4-5, 95-96
Gulick, Margaret 4
Gutkind, Peter Claus Wolfgang 5, 24, 47, 109, 114
Gutman, Robert 96

H

Haavio-Mannila Elina 96
Halberstein, R. A. 59-60
Halstrom, Engin Inel 25
Hammel, Eugene A. 25
Harblin, Thomas Devaney 25-26
Hareven, Tamara K. 38, 60
Harkess, Shirley J. 96
Harries-Jones, Peter 26
Harris, Christopher 44
Hart, Donn V. 5-6
Hashmi, Sultan H. 60
Hass, Paula H. 79-80
Hatt, Paul K. 60
Hauser, Philip Morris 6, 26-27, 61, 114
Hellmann, Ellen 80
Hendershot, Gerry E. 61
Herskovits, Melville J. 84-85, 113
Hinday, Virginia Aldise 61
Holleman, J.F. 27

Author Index

TITLE INDEX

Indexed here are titles to all books, collections, proceedings, reports, and publications of associations. Journals and journal articles are not included. Doctoral dissertations are set off in quotation marks. This index is alphabetized by letter. Numbers refer to page numbers. Lengthy titles are frequently shortened but remain unaltered in any other way.

A

Africa in Transition 27
African City Life 36, 83-84, 115
African Rural-Urban Migration 2, 113
African Urban Life 86
African Women 97-98
African Women in Towns 7, 98-99, 114
African Workers in Town 12
American Doctoral Dissertations 117

B

Backgrounds of Human Fertility in Puerto Rico 60
Baumannville 9-10, 39
Behind Ghetto Walls 43
Black Carib Household Structure 3-4, 23, 114
Britain's Married Women Workers 81

C

"City, Country, and Child-Rearing" 23-24
City and Peasant 12
City in Modern Africa, The 18-19, 33, 115

City Life in Japan 20-21
Comprehensive Dissertations Index 117
Continuity and Change in African Cultures 84-85, 113
Copper Town 104, 115
Cross-National Family Research 93
Culture Change in Contemporary Africa 97
Custom and Politics in Urban Africa 2, 76-77, 113-14

D

"Demographic Analysis of Urbanization, A" 3
Dissertation Abstracts International 117

E

Economic and Social Change 2, 18
"Effect on Family Structure of Changing Economic Activities of Women in a Gold Coast Town, The" 82

F

Families Against the City 45

Title Index

Title Index

V

Victorian City, The 47–48, 51, 114

W

Wage Earning Women 83
West African City 1
West African Urbanization 99–100, 114
Widowhood in an American City 35, 115
Woman's Work in Municipalities 92
Women: A Comparative Study 11–12, 89, 110–11
Women and World Development 10, 12–13, 115
Women in China 71, 86

Women in Contemporary India 48, 102, 114
Women in the New Asia 90, 116
Women in the Twentieth Century 93
Women in the Working Force of India 79
"Women of Accra" 103
Women's Role in Economic Development 75–76, 113
Women's Studies Abstracts 117
World Conference of the International Women's Year 77–78, 106–7

Y

Yoruba Towns and Cities 81, 114

SUBJECT INDEX

Indexed here are the major areas within the subject. This index is alphabetized letter by letter. Numbers refer to page numbers.

Subject Index

Subject Index

Urban women, repubation p. xi, 2, 5, 12, 101, 109–11

V

Venezuela 53, 79–80, 88
Vietnam 90

W

West Africa 1, 8–9, 28, 46, 77–78, 81–83, 99–100
West Germany 35
Widows 3, 6–7, 9–10, 34–35, 38, 42, 47, 52, 64, 79, 94
Wilmington, Delaware 58–59
Women, abandoned 6–7, 25, 31, 33–34, 76–77
Women and reform activity p. xi, 20, 39, 92–93, 103
Women as traders p. xi, 7–12, 33, 36–37, 46, 76–79, 82–85
  See also Employment, female in Africa

Womens organizations, urban p. xi, 10, 20, 80, 93, 97–103, 107
World War Two p. xi

Y

Yoruba 1, 7–8, 28, 36–37, 39–40, 46, 76–77, 81–82
Young women in cities 5, 8–9, 31–32
Yugoslavia 20, 88, 110

X

Xhosa 42, 101

Z

Zambia 11
Zanzibar Protectorate 52
Zulus 9–10, 16